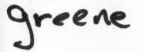

Recognized as an
American National Standard (ANSI)

IEEE
Std 802.1D-1990

IEEE Standards for
Local and Metropolitan Area Networks:

Media Access Control (MAC) Bridges

Sponsor

**Technical Committee on Computer Communications
of the
IEEE Computer Society**

Approved May 31, 1990

IEEE Standards Board

Approved October 18, 1990

American National Standards Institute

Abstract: IEEE 802.1D-1990, *IEEE Standards for Local and Metropolitan Area Networks: Media Access Control (MAC) Bridges*, defines an architecture for the interconnection of IEEE 802 Local Area Networks (LANs) below the level of the MAC Service, transparent to LLC and higher layer protocols. The operation and management of the connecting Bridges is specified. A Spanning Tree Algorithm and Protocol ensures a loop-free topology and provides redundancy. The Bridging method is not particular to any MAC type—criteria for additional MAC-specific Bridging methods are defined.

ISBN 1-55937-055-6
Library of Congress Catalog Card Number 91-070212

Copyright © 1991 by

**The Institute of Electrical and Electronics Engineers, Inc.
345 East 47th Street, New York, NY 10017-2394, USA**

March 8, 1991   *SH13565*

IEEE Standards documents are developed within the Technical Committees of the IEEE Societies and the Standards Coordinating Committees of the IEEE Standards Board. Members of the committees serve voluntarily and without compensation. They are not necessarily members of the Institute. The standards developed within IEEE represent a consensus of the broad expertise on the subject within the Institute as well as those activities outside of IEEE which have expressed an interest in participating in the development of the standard.

Use of an IEEE Standard is wholly voluntary. The existence of an IEEE Standard does not imply that there are no other ways to produce, test, measure, purchase, market, or provide other goods and services related to the scope of the IEEE Standard. Furthermore, the viewpoint expressed at the time a standard is approved and issued is subject to change brought about through developments in the state of the art and comments received from users of the standard. Every IEEE Standard is subjected to review at least once every five years for revision or reaffirmation. When a document is more than five years old, and has not been reaffirmed, it is reasonable to conclude that its contents, although still of some value, do not wholly reflect the present state of the art. Users are cautioned to check to determine that they have the latest edition of any IEEE Standard.

Comments for revision of IEEE Standards are welcome from any interested party, regardless of membership affiliation with IEEE. Suggestions for changes in documents should be in the form of a proposed change of text, together with appropriate supporting comments.

Interpretations: Occasionally questions may arise regarding the meaning of portions of standards as they relate to specific applications. When the need for interpretations is brought to the attention of IEEE, the Institute will initiate action to prepare appropriate responses. Since IEEE Standards represent a consensus of all concerned interests, it is important to ensure that any interpretation has also received the concurrence of a balance of interests. For this reason IEEE and the members of its technical committees are not able to provide an instant response to interpretation requests except in those cases where the matter has previously received formal consideration.

Comments on standards and requests for interpretations should be addressed to:

Secretary, IEEE Standards Board
P.O. Box 1331
445 Hoes Lane
Piscataway, NJ 08855-1331
USA

Foreword

(This Foreword is not a part of IEEE Std 802.1D-1990, IEEE Standards for Local and Metropolitan Area Networks: Media Access Control (MAC) Bridges.)

This standard is part of a family of standards for Local and Metropolitan Area Networks. The relationship between this standard and other members of the family is shown below. (The numbers in the figure refer to IEEE Standard numbers.)

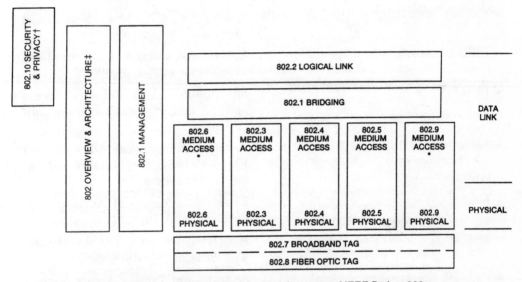

*   802.6 and 802.9 provide services beyond the scope of IEEE Project 802.

†   802.10 is co-sponsored by the Technical Committee on Computer Communications (which sponsors Project 802) and also the Technical Committee on Security and Privacy.

‡   Formerly IEEE Std 802.1A.

Relationship Among IEEE Project 802 Working Groups and Technical Advisory Groups

The family of IEEE 802 Standards includes publications, projects, and activities that define standards, recommended practices, and guidelines in the following areas:

- IEEE Std 802*:   Overview and Architecture. This document forms part of the 802.1 scope of work.

---

*The 802 Architecture and Overview Specification, originally known as IEEE Std 802.1A, has been renumbered as IEEE Std 802. This has been done to accommodate recognition of the base standard in a family of standards. References to IEEE Std 802.1A should be considered as references to IEEE Std 802.

- IEEE 802.1 series: Glossary, Network Management, and Internetworking. These documents, as well as IEEE Std 802, Overview and Architecture, form part of the 802.1 scope of work.

- ISO 8802-2 [ANSI/IEEE Std 802.2]: Logical Link Control

- ISO/IEC 8802-3 [ANSI/IEEE Std 802.3]: CSMA/CD Access Method and Physical Layer Specifications

- ISO/IEC 8802-4 [ANSI/IEEE Std 802.4]: Token-Passing Bus Access Method and Physical Layer Specifications

- IEEE Std 802.5: Token-Passing Ring Access Method and Physical Layer Specifications

- P802.6: Metropolitan Area Network Access Method and Physical Layer Specifications

- IEEE Std 802.7: Broadband Technical Advisory and Physical Layer Topics and Recommended Practices

- P802.8: Fiber Optic Technical Advisory and Physical Layer Topics

- P802.9: Integrated Voice/Data Access Method and Physical Layer Specifications

- P802.10: Security and Privary Access Method and Physcial Layer Specifications

- P802.11: Wireless Access Method and Physical Layer Specification (activity on this project began as this document went to press)

This document, IEEE Std 802.1D, specifies an architecture and protocol for the interconnection of IEEE 802 LANs below the MAC service boundary.

The reader of this document is urged to become familiar with the complete family of standards.

Readers wishing to know the state of revision should contact the 802.1 Working Group Chair via

Secretary
IEEE Standards Board
Institute of Electrical and Electronics Engineers, Inc.
445 Hoes Lane, P.O. Box 1331
Piscataway, NJ 08855-1331

The following is an alphabetical list of participants in the IEEE Project 802.1 Working Group:

William P. Lidinsky, *Chair**
Mick Seaman, *Chair, Interworking Task Group**

Fumio Akashi	Pat Gonia	Ron L. G. Prince
Ann Ambler	Richard Graham*	Nigel Ramsden
Paul D. Amer	Michael A. Gravel	Trudy Reusser
Charles Arnold	Mogens Hansen	Edouard Rocher
Floyd Backes*	Harold Harrington	Paul Rosenblum*
Ann Ballard	John Hart*	John Salter
Richard Bantel	Mike Harvey*	Alan Sarsby
Sy Bederman	Bob Herbst	Susan Schanning
Amatzia Ben-Artzi	Jack R. Hung	Gerry Segal*
Robert Bledsoe	Thomas Hytry	Rich Seifert*
Kwame Boakye	Jay Israel	Howard Sherry
Frank Bruns	Tony Jeffree*	Wu-Shi Shung
Juan Bulnes	Hal Keen*	M. Soha
Fred Burg	Alan Kirby	Dan Stokesberry
Peter Carbone	Kimberly Kirkpatrick	Lennart Swartz
Alan Chambers*	Steve Kleiman	Kenta Takumi
Ken Chapman	James Kristof*	Robin Tasker*
Alice Chen	H. Eugene Latham*	Angus Telfer
Jade Chien	Bing Liao*	Dave Thompson
Jim Corrigan	Andy Luque	Nathan Tobol
Paul Cowell*	George Lin*	Wendell Turner
Peter Dawe	Phillip Magnuson	Peter Videcrantz*
Stan Degen*	Bruce McClure	Paul Wainright
Frank Deignan	Tom McGowan	Scott Wasson*
Ron Dhondy	Margaret A. Merrick	Daniel Watts
Eiji Doi	Jim Montrose	Alan Weissberger
Barbara J. Don Carlos	Jerry O'Keefe	Deborah Wilbert
Walter Eldon	Richard Patti*	Val Wilson
Eldon D. Feist	Roger Pfister*	Igor Zhovnirovsky*
Len Fishler*	Thomas L. Phinney	Carolyn Zimmer*
Kevin Flanagan*	Daniel Pitt*	Nick Zucchero

*Voting member of the 802.1 Working Group at the time of approval of this document.

The following persons were on the balloting committee that approved this document for submission to the IEEE Standards Board:

When the IEEE Standards Board approved this standard on May 31, 1990, it had the following membership:

Contents

IEEE Standards for
Local and Metropolitan Area Networks:

Media Access Control (MAC) Bridges

1. Introduction

IEEE 802 Local Area Networks (LANs) of all types may be connected together with media access control (MAC) Bridges. Each individual LAN has its own independent MAC. The Bridged Local Area Network created allows the interconnection of stations attached to separate LANs as if they were attached to a single LAN. A MAC Bridge operates below the MAC Service Boundary, and is transparent to protocols operating above this boundary, in the Logical Link Control (LLC) Sublayer or Network Layer (ISO 7498:1984 [9][1]). A Bridged Local Area Network may provide for the following:

(1) The interconnection of stations attached to 802 LANs of different MAC types.
(2) An effective increase in the physical extent, the number of permissible attachments, or the total performance of a LAN.
(3) Partitioning of the physical LAN support for administrative or maintenance reasons.

1.1 Scope. For the purpose of compatible interconnection of data processing equipment using the IEEE 802 MAC Service supported by interconnected IEEE 802 Standard Local Area Networks of various types, this standard specifies the operation of MAC Bridges. To this end it

(1) Positions the bridging function within an architectural description of the MAC Sublayer.

---

[1] The numbers in brackets correspond to those of the references listed in 1.4.

(2) Defines the principles of operation of the MAC Bridge in terms of the support and preservation of the MAC Service, and the maintenance of Quality of Service.

(3) Specifies the MAC Internal Sublayer Service provided by individual LANs to the Media Access Method Independent Functions that provide frame relay in the Bridge.

(4) Identifies the functions to be performed by Bridges, and provides an architectural model of the internal operation of a Bridge in terms of Processes and Entities that provide those functions.

(5) Establishes the requirements for a protocol between the Bridges in a Bridged Local Area Network to configure the network, and specifies the distributed computation of a Spanning Tree active topology.

(6) Specifies the encoding of the Bridge Protocol Data Units (BPDUs).

(7) Establishes the requirements for Bridge Management in the Bridged Local Area Network, identifying the managed objects and defining the management operations.

(8) Specifies how the management operations are made available to a remote manager using the protocol and architectural description provided by P802.1B [3].

(9) Specifies performance requirements and recommends default values and applicable ranges for the operational parameters of a Bridge.

(10) Specifies the requirements to be satisfied by equipment claiming conformance to this standard.

(11) Specifies criteria for the use of MAC-specific bridging methods.

This standard specifies the operation of MAC Bridges that attach directly to LANs as specified in the relevant MAC standards for the MAC technology or technologies implemented. The specification of Remote Bridges, which interconnect LANs using Wide Area Network (WAN) media for the transmission of frames between Bridges, is outside the scope of this standard.

1.2 Definition. The following definition is specific to this standard:

Bridged Local Area Network. A catanet of individual Local Area Networks interconnected by MAC Bridges.

1.3 Abbreviation. The following abbreviation is specific to this standard:

BPDU. Bridge Protocol Data Unit.

1.4 References. This standard shall be used in conjunction with the following pubications or their approved revisions:

[1] ANSI X3.159-1989, American National Standards for Information Systems — Programming Language — C.[2]

---

[2] ANSI publications are available from the Sales Department, American National Standards Institute, 1430 Broadway, New York, NY 10018.

[2] IEEE Std 802-1990, IEEE Standards for Local and Metropolitan Area Networks: Overview and Architecture.

[3] Reserved for future use.[3]

[4] ISO 8802-2:1989 [ANSI/IEEE Std 802.2-1989], Information processing systems—Local area networks—Part 2: Logical link control.[4]

[5] ISO/IEC 8802-3:1990 [ANSI/IEEE Std 802.3-1990 Edition], Information processing systems—Local area networks—Part 3: Carrier sense multiple access with collision detection (CSMA/CD) access method and physical layer specifications.

[6] ISO/IEC 8802-4:1990 [ANSI/IEEE Std 802.4-1990], Information processing systems—Local area networks—Part 4: Token-passing bus access method and physical layer specifications.

[7] IEEE Std 802.5-1989, IEEE Standards for Local Area Networks: Token Ring Access Method and Physical Layer Specifications.

[8] ISO 6937-2:1983, Information processing—Coded character sets for text communication—Part 2: Latin alphabetic and non-alphabetic graphic characters.[5]

[9] ISO 7498:1984, Information processing systems—Open Systems Interconnection—Basic Reference Model.

[10] ISO 8824:1987, Information processing systems—Open Systems Interconnection—Specification of Abstract Syntax Notation One (ASN.1).

[11] ISO 8825:1987, Information processing systems—Open Systems Interconnection—Specification of Basic Encoding Rules for Abstract Syntax Notation One (ASN.1).

[12] ISO/IEC 9595:1990, Information processing systems—Open Systems Interconnection—Common management information service definition.

[13] ISO/IEC 9596:1990, Information processing systems—Open Systems Interconnection—Common management information protocol specification.

---

[3] When the following IEEE project is approved, it will become a part of this reference section: P802.1B, LAN/MAN Management. Available from IEEE Computer Society Documents, c/o AlphaGraphics, ATTN: P. Thrush, 10215 N. 35th Ave., Suite A & B, Phoenix, AZ 85051.

[4] ISO [IEEE] and ISO/IEC [IEEE] documents are available from ISO Central Secretariat, 1 rue de Varembé, Case Postale 56, CH-1211, Genève 20, Switzerland/Suisse; and from the Service Center, Institute of Electrical and Electronics Engineers, 445 Hoes Lane, P.O. Box 1331, Piscataway, NJ 08855-1331.

[5] ISO and ISO/IEC documents are available from the ISO Central Secretariat, 1 rue de Varembé, Case Postale 56, CH-1211, Genève 20, Switzerland/Suisse; and from the Sales Department, American National Standards Institute, 1430 Broadway, New York, NY 10018, USA.

1.5 Conformance. A MAC Bridge that claims conformance to this standard

(1) Shall conform to

  (a) The relevant MAC standards for the MAC technology or technologies implemented, i.e., ISO/IEC 8802-3 [5], ISO/IEC 8802-4 [6], or IEEE Std 802.5 [7], as described in 2.5, and

  (b) ISO 8802-2:1989 [4] for the implementation of a Class I or Class II LLC, to support Type 1 operation as required by 3.2, 3.3, and 3.12.

(2) Shall relay and filter frames as described in 3.1 and specified in 3.5, 3.6, and 3.7.

(3) Shall either

  (a) Filter frames with equal source and destination addresses, or

  (b) Not filter frames with equal source and destination addresses, as specified in 3.7.

(4) May provide the capability to control the mapping of the priority of forwarded frames as specified in 3.7.

(5) Shall maintain the information required to make frame-filtering decisions as described in 3.1 and specified in 3.8 and 3.9.

(6) Shall use stated values of the following parameters of the Filtering Database (3.9):

  (a) Filtering Database Size, the maximum number of entries that can be held in the Filtering Database.

  (b) Permanent Database Size, the maximum number of entries that can be held in the Permanent Database.

(7) May provide the capability to read and update the Filtering and Permanent Databases as specified in 3.9.

(8) May provide the capability to set the Ageing Time as specified in 3.9. A Bridge that provides this capability shall implement the full range of values specified in Table 3-3.

(9) Shall use either

  (a) 48-bit Universally Administered Addresses, or

  (b) 48-bit Locally Administered Addresses, or

  (c) 16-bit Locally Administered Addresses, as specified in 3.12.

(10) Shall conform to the provisions for addressing specified in 3.12.

(11) May implement the optional provisions for addressing Bridge Management as specified in 3.12.4, for associating the Bridge Address with a Bridge Port as specified in 3.12.5, and for preconfiguring group addresses in the Permanent Database as specified in 3.12.6.

(12) Shall provide

  (a) A means of assigning a group MAC Address to identify the Bridge Protocol Entity if 48-bit Universally Administered Addresses are not used, and

  (b) A means of assigning an address unique within a Bridged Local Area Network to uniquely identify the Bridge if 16-bit Locally Administered Addresses are used, as specified in 4.5, and

  (c) A distinct Port identifier for each Port of the Bridge, as specified in 4.5, as required by 4.2 for operation of the Spanning Tree Algorithm and Protocol.

(13) Shall implement the Spanning Tree Algorithm and Protocol described in Section 4, as specified in 4.7.

(14) Shall not exceed the values given in 4.10.2 for the following parameters:

(a) Maximum bridge transit delay

(b) Maximum Message Age increment overestimate

(c) Maximum BPDU transmission delay

(15) Shall use the value given in Table 4-3 for the following parameter:

(a) Hold Timer

(16) May provide the capability to assign values to the following parameters to allow configuration of the Spanning Tree active topology:

(a) Bridge Priority

(b) Port Priority

(c) Path Cost for each Port

A Bridge that provides this capability shall implement the range of values specified in 4.10.2 and Tables 4-4 and 4-5.

(17) May provide the capability to set the values of the following parameters of the Spanning Tree Algorithm and Protocol:

(a) Bridge Max Age

(b) Bridge Hello Time

(c) Bridge Forward Delay

A Bridge that provides this capability shall implement the range of values specified in 4.10.2 and Table 4-3.

(18) Shall encode transmitted BPDUs and validate received BPDUs as specified in Section 5.

(19) May support management of the Bridge. Bridges claiming to support management shall support all the management objects and operations defined in Section 6.

(20) May support IEEE 802.1 remote management. Bridges claiming to support IEEE 802.1 remote management shall

(a) Conform to P802.1B [3].

(b) Support remote management by the use of the network management operations and encodings specified in Section 7.

(21) Shall specify a Guaranteed Port Filtering Rate for each Bridge Port, a Guaranteed Bridge Relaying Rate for the Bridge, and the related time intervals T_F and T_R as specified in Section 8. Operation of the Bridge within the specified parameters shall not violate any of the other conformance provisions of this Standard.

The supplier of an implementation that is claimed to conform to this standard shall complete a copy of the PICS proforma provided in Appendix A and shall provide the information necessary to identify both the supplier and the implementation.

1.6 Recommendations

1.6.1 Management. Support of the managed objects and management operations specified in Section 6 is highly recommended.

1.7 MAC-specific Bridging Methods. MAC-specific bridging methods may exist. Use of a MAC-specific bridging method and the method specified in this standard on the same LAN shall

(1) Not prevent communication between stations in a Bridged Local Area Network.

(2) Preserve the MAC Service.

(3) Preserve the characteristics of each bridging method within its own domain.

(4) Provide for the ability of both bridging techniques to coexist simultaneously on a LAN without adverse interaction.

2. Support of the MAC Service

MAC Bridges interconnect the separate LANs that comprise a Bridged Local Area Network by relaying frames between the separate MACs of the bridged LANs. The position of the bridging function within the MAC Sublayer is shown in Fig 2-1.

The MAC Service is provided to the MAC Service User in the end stations and is supported by the relay function in the Bridge. This may exclude features specific to individual medium access technologies.

This section discusses provision of the MAC Service to end stations, support of the MAC Service by Bridges, preservation of the MAC Service offered by the Bridged Local Area Network, maintenance of Quality of Service in the Bridged Local Area Network, and the Internal Sublayer Service offered to Bridges themselves to enable them to connect individual LANs.

2.1 Support of the MAC Service. The MAC Service provided to end stations attached to a Bridged Local Area Network is supported by the Bridges in that Bridged Local Area Network. Bridges support MA_UNITDATA.request primitives and corresponding MA_UNITDATA.indication primitives conveying user data with unconfirmed service. The use of confirmed service by end stations communicating across a Bridge is not supported.

The style of Bridge operation maximizes the availability of the MAC Service to end stations and assists in the maintenance of the Bridged Local Area Network. It is therefore desirable that Bridges be capable of being configured in the Bridged Local Area Network:

(1) So as to provide redundant paths between end stations to enable the Bridged Local Area Network to continue to provide the Service in the event of component failure (of Bridge or LAN).

(2) So that the paths supported between end stations are predictable and configurable given the availability of Bridged Local Area Network components.

2.2 Preservation of the MAC Service. The MAC Service offered by a Bridged Local Area Network consisting of LANs interconnected by MAC Bridges is similar (2.3) to that offered by a single LAN. In consequence,

(1) A Bridge is not directly addressed by communicating end stations, except as an end station for management purposes: frames transmitted between end stations carry the MAC Address of the peer-end station in their Destination Address field, not the MAC Address, if any, of the Bridge.

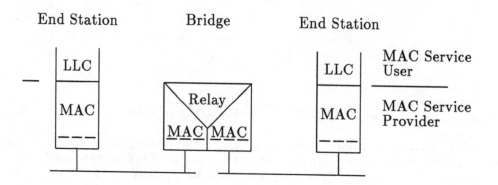

Fig 2-1
Internal Organization of the MAC Sublayer

(2) All MAC Addresses must be unique and addressable within the Bridged Local Area Network.

(3) The MAC Addresses of end stations are not restricted by the topology and configuration of the Bridged Local Area Network.

2.3 Quality of Service Maintenance. The quality of the MAC Service supported by a Bridge should not be significantly inferior to that provided by a single LAN. The Quality of Service parameters to be considered are those which relate to

(1) Service availability
(2) Frame loss
(3) Frame misordering
(4) Frame duplication
(5) The transit delay experienced by frames
(6) Frame lifetime
(7) The undetected frame error rate
(8) Maximum service data unit size supported
(9) User priority
(10) Throughput

2.3.1 Service Availability. The MAC Sublayer provides the MAC Service to end stations attached to a LAN or a Bridged Local Area Network. Service availability is measured as that fraction of some total time during which the service is provided. The operation of a Bridge can increase or lower the service availability.

The service availability can be increased by automatic reconfiguration of the Bridged Local Area Network in order to avoid the use of a failed component (e.g., repeater, cable, or connector) in the data path. The service availability can be lowered by failure of a Bridge itself, through denial of service by the Bridge, or through frame filtering by the Bridge.

A Bridge may deny service and discard frames (2.3.2) in order to preserve other aspects of the MAC Service (2.3.3; 2.3.4) when automatic reconfiguration takes place. Service may be denied to end stations that do not benefit from the reconfiguration; hence, the service availability is lowered for those end stations. Bridges may filter frames in order to localize traffic in the Bridged Local Area Network. Should an end station move, it may then be unable to receive frames from other end stations until the filtering information held by the Bridges is updated.

To maximize the service availability, no loss of service or delay in service provision should be caused by Bridges, except as a consequence of a failure, removal, or insertion of a Bridged Local Area Network component, or as a consequence of the movement of an end station. These are regarded as extraordinary events. The operation of any additional protocol necessary to maintain the quality of the MAC Service is thus limited to the configuration of the Bridged Local Area Network, and is independent of individual instances of service provision.

2.3.2 Frame Loss. The service provided by the MAC Sublayer does not guarantee the delivery of Service Data Units. Frames transmitted by a source station arrive, uncorrupted, at the destination station with high probability. The operation of a Bridge introduces minimal additional frame loss.

A frame transmitted by a source station can fail to reach its destination station as a result of

(1) Frame corruption during physical layer transmission or reception.
(2) Frame discard by a Bridge because
    (a) It is unable to transmit them within some maximum time and, hence, must discard the frame to prevent the maximum frame lifetime (2.3.6) being exceeded.
    (b) It is unable to continue to store the frame due to exhaustion of internal buffering capacity as frames continue to arrive at a rate in excess of that at which they can be transmitted.
    (c) The size of the service data unit carried by the frame exceeds the maximum supported by the medium access control procedures employed on the LAN to which the frame is to be relayed.
    (d) Changes in the connected topology of the Bridged Local Area Network necessitate frame discard for a limited period of time to maintain other aspects of Quality of Service.

2.3.3 Frame Misordering. The service provided by the MAC Sublayer does not permit the reordering of frames transmitted with a given user priority. MA_UNITDATA.indication service primitives corresponding to MA_UNITDATA.request primitives with the same requested priority are received in the same order as the request primitives were processed. The operation of the Bridges does not misorder frames transmitted with the same user priority.

Where Bridges in a Bridged Local Area Network are capable of connecting the individual MACs in such a way that multiple paths between any source station–destination station pairs exist, the operation of a protocol is required to ensure that multiple paths do not occur.

2.3.4 Frame Duplication. The service provided by the MAC Sublayer does not permit the duplication of frames. The operation of Bridges does not introduce duplication of user data frames.

The potential for frame duplication in a Bridged Local Area Network arises through the possibility of duplication of received frames on subsequent transmission within a Bridge, or through the possibility of multiple paths between source and destination end stations.

A Bridge shall not duplicate user data frames.

2.3.5 Transit Delay. The service provided by the MAC Sublayer introduces a frame transit delay that is dependent on the particular media and media access control method employed. Frame transit delay is the elapsed time between an MA_UNITDATA.request primitive and the corresponding MA_UNITDATA.indication primitive. Elapsed time values are calculated only on Service Data Units that are successfully transferred.

Since the MAC Service is provided at an abstract interface within an end station, it is not possible to specify precisely the total frame transit delay. It is, however, possible to measure those components of delay associated with media access and with transmission and reception; and the transit delay introduced by an intermediate system, in this case a Bridge, can be measured.

The minimum additional transit delay introduced by a Bridge is the time taken to receive a frame plus that taken to access the media onto which the frame is to be relayed. Note that the frame is completely received before it is relayed as the Frame Check Sequence (FCS) is to be calculated and the frame discarded if in error.

2.3.6 Frame Lifetime. The service provided by the MAC Sublayer ensures that there is an upper bound to the transit delay experienced for a particular instance of communication. This maximum frame lifetime is necessary to ensure the correct operation of higher layer protocols. The additional transit delay introduced by a Bridge is discussed above.

To enforce the maximum frame lifetime a Bridge may be required to discard frames. Since the information provided by the MAC Sublayer to a Bridge does not include the transit delay already experienced by any particular frame, Bridges must discard frames to enforce a maximum delay in each Bridge.

The value of the maximum bridge transit delay is based on both the maximum delays imposed by all the Bridges in the Bridged Local Area Network and the desired maximum frame lifetime. A recommended and an absolute maximum value are specified in Table 4-2.

2.3.7 Undetected Frame Error Rate. The service provided by the MAC Sublayer introduces a very low undetected frame error rate in transmitted frames. Undetected errors are protected against by the use of a FCS that is appended to the frame by the MAC Sublayer of the source station prior to transmission, and checked by the destination station on reception.

The FCS calculated for a given Service Data Unit is dependent on the medium access control method employed. It is therefore necessary to recalculate the FCS within a Bridge providing a relay function between IEEE 802 MACs of dissimilar types. This introduces the possibility of additional undetected errors arising from the operation of a Bridge. For frames relayed between LANs of the same MAC type, the Bridge shall not introduce an undetected frame error rate greater than that which would be achieved by preserving the FCS.

2.3.8 Maximum Service Data Unit Size. The Maximum Service Data Unit Size that can be supported by an IEEE 802 LAN varies with the media access control method and its associated parameters (speed, etc.). It may be constrained by the owner of the LAN.

The Maximum Service Data Unit Size supported by a Bridge between two LANs is the smaller of that supported by the LANs. No attempt is made by a Bridge to relay a frame to a LAN that does not support the size of Service Data Unit conveyed by that frame.

2.3.9 Priority. The service provided by the MAC Sublayer includes user priority as a Quality of Service parameter. MA_UNITDATA.request primitives with a high priority may be given precedence over other request primitives made at the same station, or at other stations attached to the same LAN, and can give rise to earlier MA_UNITDATA.indication primitives.

The MAC Sublayer maps the requested user priorities onto the access priorities supported by the individual medium access control method. The requested user priority may be conveyed to the destination station.

Since a Bridge shall not reorder frames originating from MA_UNITDATA.request primitives of the same user priority, the mapping of priority must be static.

2.3.10 Throughput. The total throughput provided by a Bridged Local Area Network can be significantly greater than that provided by an equivalent single LAN. Bridges may localize traffic within the Bridged Local Area Network by filtering frames.

The throughput between end stations on individual LANs, communicating through a Bridge, can be lowered by frame discard in the Bridge due to the inability to transmit at the required rate on the LAN forming the path to the destination for an extended period.

2.4 Internal Sublayer Service Provided within the MAC Bridge. The Internal Sublayer Service provided by the MAC entities to the MAC Relay Entity within a Bridge is that provided by the individual, independent MACs. The Bridge observes the appropriate MAC procedures and protocol for each LAN to which it is connected. No control frames (also known as MAC frames) that govern the operation of an individual LAN are forwarded off the LAN of their origin.

The Internal Sublayer Service excludes MAC specific features and procedures whose operation is confined to that of the individual LANs. The unit-data primitives that describe this service are

M_UNITDATA.indication (
                  frame_type,
                  mac_action,
                  destination_address,
                  source_address,
                  mac_service_data_unit,
                  user_priority,
                  frame_check_sequence
)

Each data indication primitive invoked corresponds to the receipt of a MAC frame from an individual LAN.

The frame_type parameter indicates the class of frame. The value of this parameter is one of user_data_frame, mac_specific_frame, or reserved_frame.

The mac_action parameter indicates the action requested of a MAC entity receiving the indication. If the value of the frame_type parameter is user_data_frame, then the mac_action parameter is one of request_with_response, request_with_no_response, or response. For mac_specific_frames and reserved_frames, this parameter does not apply.

The destination_address parameter is either the address of an individual MAC entity or a group of MAC entities.

The source_address parameter is the individual address of the source MAC entity.

The mac_service_data_unit parameter is the service user data.

The user_priority parameter is the priority requested by the originating service user. The value of this parameter, if specified, is in the range 0 (lowest) through 7 (highest).

The frame_check_sequence parameter is explicitly provided as a parameter of the primitive so that it can be used as a parameter to a related request primitive without recalculation.

The identification of the LAN from which particular frames are received is a local matter and is not expressed as a parameter of the service primitive.

```
M_UNITDATA.request  (
                    frame_type,
                    mac_action,
                    destination_address,
                    source_address,
                    mac_service_data_unit,
                    user_priority,
                    access_priority,
                    frame_check_sequence
                    )
```

A data request primitive is invoked to transmit a frame to an individual LAN.

The frame_type parameter indicates the class of frame.

The mac_action parameter indicates the action requested of the destination MAC entity.

The destination_address parameter is either the address of an individual MAC entity, or a group of MAC entities.

The source_address parameter is the individual address of the source MAC entity.

The mac_service_data_unit parameter is the service user data.

The user_priority parameter is the priority requested by the originating service user. The value of this parameter, if specified, is in the range 0 (lowest) through 7 (highest).

The access_priority parameter is the priority used by the local service provider to convey the request. It can be used to determine the priority attached to the transmission of frames queued by the local MAC Entity, both locally and amongst other stations attached to the same individual LAN—if the media access method permits. The value of this parameter, if specified, is in the range 0 (lowest) through 7 (highest).

The frame_check_sequence parameter is explicitly provided as a parameter of the primitive so that it can be used without recalculation.

The identification of the LAN to which a frame is to be transmitted is a local matter and is not expressed as a parameter of the service primitive.

2.5 Support of the Internal Sublayer Service by Specific MAC Procedures. This section specifies the mapping of the Internal Sublayer Service to the MAC Protocol and Procedures of each individual IEEE 802 MAC type, and the encoding of the parameters of the service in MAC frames. The mapping is specified by reference to the IEEE 802 Standards that specify the individual media access methods. The mapping draws attention to any special responsibilities of Bridges attached to LANs of that MAC type.

2.5.1 Support by ISO/IEC 8802-3 [5] (CSMA/CD). The CSMA/CD access method is specified in ISO/IEC 8802-3 [5]. Section 3 of that standard specifies the media access control frame structure, and Section 4 specifies the media access control method.

On receipt of an M_UNITDATA.request primitive, the local MAC Entity performs Transmit Data Encapsulation, assembling a frame using the parameters supplied as specified below. It appends a preamble and a Start Frame Delimiter before handing the frame to the Transmit Media Access Management Component in the MAC Sublayer for transmission ([5], 4.2.3).

On receipt of a MAC frame by Receive Media Access Management, the MAC frame is passed to Receive Data Decapsulation which validates the FCS and disassembles the frame, as specified below, into the parameters that are supplied with an M_UNITDATA.indication primitive ([5], 4.2.4).

The frame_type parameter only takes the value user_data_frame and is not explicitly encoded in MAC frames.

The mac_action parameter only takes the value request_with_no_response and is not explicitly encoded in MAC frames.

The destination_address parameter is encoded in the destination address field of the MAC frame ([5], 3.2.3).

The source_address parameter is encoded in the source address field of the MAC frame ([5], 3.2.3).

The number of octets in the mac_service_data_unit parameter is encoded in the length field of the MAC frame ([5], 3.2.6), and the octets of data are encoded in the data field ([5], 3.2.7).

The user_priority parameter is not encoded in MAC frames and takes the value unspecified on corresponding M_UNITDATA.indication primitives.

The frame_check_sequence parameter is encoded in the FCS field of the MAC frame ([5], 3.2.8). The FCS is computed as a function of the destination address, source address, length, data and pad fields. This parameter, therefore, also conveys the value of the PAD field necessary to meet the requirement for a minimum frame size ([5], 3.2.7). If an M_UNITDATA.request primitive is not accompanied by this parameter, it is calculated in accordance with [5], 3.2.8.

No special action, above that specified for the support of use of the MAC Service by LLC, is required for the support of the MAC Internal Sublayer Service by the CSMA/CD access method.

2.5.2 Support by ISO/IEC 8802-4 [6] (Token-Passing Bus). The token-passing bus access method is specified in ISO/IEC 8802-4 [6]. Section 4 of that standard specifies frame formats. Section 5 discusses the basic concepts of the access protocols, and Section 7 provides the definitive specification of the token-passing bus MAC operation.

On receipt of an M_UNITDATA.request primitive the local MAC Entity Interface Machine (IFM) queues a frame for transmission by the Access Control Machine (ACM) ([6], Section 7). On transmission the frame fields are set using the parameters supplied as specified below, and the Preamble, Start Delimiter, and End Delimiter are added ([6], Section 4).

On receipt of a valid MAC frame by the Receive Machine (RxM) ([6], 7.1.5), an M_UNITDATA.indication primitive is generated, with parameters derived from the frame fields as specified below.

The frame_type parameter is encoded in the FF bits (bit positions 1 and 2) of the frame control field ([6], 4.1.3.1, 4.1.3.2). A bit pattern of 0 1 denotes a user_data_ frame, a bit pattern of 0 0 or 1 0 denotes a mac_specific_frame, and a bit pattern of 1 1 denotes a reserved_frame.

The mac_action parameter is encoded in the MMM bits (bit positions 3, 4, and 5) of the frame control field ([6], 4.1.3.2). For user_data_frames these take the values 0 0 0 for request_with_no_response, 0 0 1 for request_with_response, and 0 1 0 for response.

The destination_address parameter is encoded in the destination address field of the MAC frame ([6], 4.1.4.1).

The source_address parameter is encoded in the source address field of the MAC frame ([6], 4.1.4.2).

The mac_service_data_unit parameter is encoded in the MAC Data Unit field ([6], 4.1.5).

The user_priority parameter is encoded in the PPP bits (bit positions 6, 7, and 8) of the frame control field ([6], 4.1.3.2; [6], 5.1.7).

The frame_check_sequence parameter is encoded in the FCS field of the MAC frame ([6], 4.1.6). The FCS is computed as a function of the frame control, destination address, source address, and data fields. If an M_UNITDATA.request primitive is not accompanied by this parameter, it is calculated in accordance with [6], 4.1.6.

No special action, above that specified for the support of use of the MAC Service by LLC, is required for the support of the MAC Internal Sublayer Service by the token-passing bus access method.

2.5.3 Support by IEEE Std 802.5 [7] (Token-Passing Ring). The token-passing ring access method is specified in IEEE Std 802.5 [7]. Section 3 of that standard specifies formats and facilities, and Section 4 specifies token-passing ring protocols.

On receipt of an M_UNITDATA.request primitive the local MAC Entity composes a frame using the parameters supplied as specified below, appending the frame control, destination address, source address, and FCS fields to the user data, and enqueuing the frame for transmission on reception of a suitable token ([7], 4.1.1). On transmission, the starting delimiter, access control field, ending delimiter, and frame status fields are added.

On receipt of a valid MAC frame ([7], 4.1.4) that was not transmitted by the Bridge Port's local MAC Entity, with the Routing Information Indicator bit (which occupies the same position in the source address field as does the Group Address bit in the destination address field) set to zero, an M_UNITDATA.indication primitive is generated, with parameters derived from the frame fields as specified below.

The frame_type parameter is encoded in the frame_type bits (FF bits) of the frame control field ([7], 3.2.3.1). A bit pattern of 0 1 denotes a user_data_frame, a bit pattern of 0 0 denotes a mac_specific_frame, and a bit pattern of 1 0 or 1 1 denotes a reserved_frame.

The mac_action parameter only takes the value request_with_no_response and is not explicitly encoded in MAC frames.

The destination_address parameter is encoded in the destination address field of the MAC frame ([7], 3.2.4.1).

The source_address parameter is encoded in the source address field of the MAC frame ([7], 3.2.4.2).

The mac_service_data_unit parameter is encoded in the information field ([7], 3.2.5).

The user_priority parameter associated with user_data_frames is encoded in the YYY bits of the frame control field ([7] 3.2.3).

The frame_check_sequence parameter is encoded in the FCS field of the MAC frame ([7], 3.2.6). The FCS is computed as a function of the frame control, destination address, source address, and information fields. If an M_UNITDATA.request primitive is not accompanied by this parameter, it is calculated in accordance with [7], 3.2.6.

The Address Recognized (A) bits in the Frame Status field of a frame ([7], 3.2.8) may be set to 1 if an M_UNITDATA.indication primitive with frame_type and mac_action parameter values of user_data_frame and request_with_no_response respectively is generated, or if such an indication would be generated if buffering had been available; otherwise the A bits shall not be set except as required by [7].

If the A bits are set to 1, the Frame Copied (C) bits ([7], 3.2.8.1) may be set to 1 to reflect the availability of receive buffering; otherwise the C bits shall not be set.

In order to support the MAC Internal Sublayer Service a Token Ring Bridge must be capable of recognizing and removing frames transmitted by itself, even though they can carry a source address different from that of the Bridge Port that transmitted them.

3. Principles of Operation

This section establishes the principles and a model of the operation of a Bridge as follows:
  (1) Explains the principal elements of Bridge operation and lists the functions that support these.
  (2) Establishes an architectural model for a Bridge that governs the provision of these functions.
  (3) Provides a model of the operation of a Bridge in terms of Processes and Entities that support the functions.
  (4) Details the addressing requirements in a Bridged Local Area Network and specifies the addressing of Entities in a Bridge.

3.1 Bridge Operation. The principal elements of Bridge operation are
  (1) Relay and filtering of frames.
  (2) Maintenance of the information required to make frame filtering and relaying decisions.
  (3) Management of the above.
  3.1.1 Relay. A MAC Bridge relays individual MAC user data frames between the separate MACs of the Bridged Local Area Networks connected to its Ports. The order of frames of given user_priority received on one Port and transmitted on another shall be preserved.

The functions that support the relaying of frames and maintain the Quality of Service supported by the Bridge are
  (1) Frame reception.
  (2) Discard on received frame in error (2.3.2).
  (3) Frame discard if the frame_type is not user_data_frame, or if its mac_action parameter is not request_with_no_response (2.4).
  (4) Frame discard following the application of filtering information.
  (5) Frame discard on transmittable service data unit size exceeded (2.3.8).
  (6) Forwarding of received frames to other Bridge Ports.
  (7) Frame discard to ensure that a maximum bridge transit delay is not exceeded (2.3.6).
  (8) Selection of outbound access priority (2.3.9).
  (9) Mapping of service data units and recalculation of Frame Check Sequence (2.3.7).
  (10) Frame transmission.

31

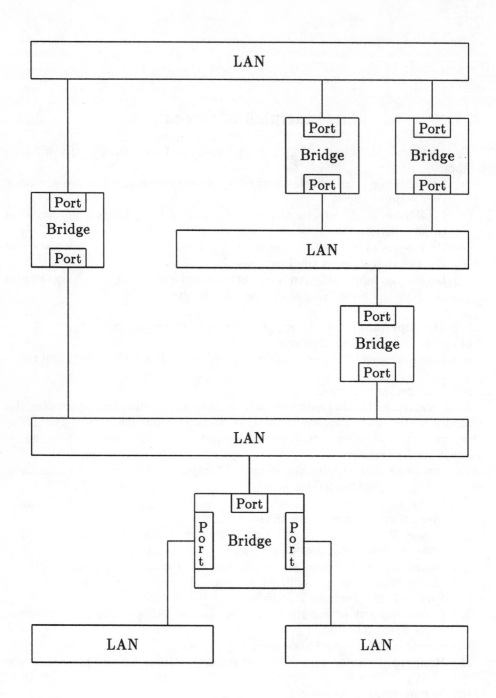

**Fig 3-1
A Bridged Local Area Network**

3.1.2 Filtering Information. A Bridge filters frames, i.e., does not relay frames received by a Bridge Port to other Ports on that Bridge, in order to prevent the duplication of frames (2.3.4). Frames transmitted between a pair of end stations can be confined to LANs that form a path between those end stations (2.3.10).

The functions that support the use and maintenance of filtering information are

(1) Permanent configuration of reserved addresses.
(2) Explicit configuration of static filtering information.
(3) Automatic learning of dynamic filtering information through observation of Bridged Local Area Network traffic.
(4) Ageing out of filtering information that has been automatically learned.
(5) Calculation and configuration of Bridged Local Area Network topology.

3.1.3 Bridge Management. The functions that support Bridge Management control and monitor the provision of the above functions. They are specified in Section 6.

3.2 Bridge Architecture. Each Bridge Port receives and transmits frames to and from the LAN to which it is attached using the services provided by the individual MAC Entity associated with that Port. The MAC Entity for each Port handles all the Media Access Method Dependent Functions (MAC protocol and procedures) as specified in the relevant IEEE 802 standard for that MAC technology.

The MAC Relay Entity handles the Media Access Method Independent Functions of relaying frames between Bridge Ports, filtering frames, and learning filtering information.

The Bridge Protocol Entity handles calculation and configuration of Bridged Local Area Network topology.

The MAC Relay Entity uses the Internal Sublayer Service provided by the separate MAC Entities for each Port. This service and its support is described in 2.4 and 2.5. It is not specific to any MAC technology.

The Bridge Protocol Entity and other higher layer protocol users, such as Bridge Management, make use of Logical Link Control procedures. These procedures are provided separately for each Port, and use the MAC Service provided by the individual MAC Entities.

Figures 3-2 and 3-3 illustrate a Bridge and its Ports and the architecture of the Bridge for a Bridge with two Ports. A Bridge may have more than two Ports.

3.3 Model of Operation. The use, by the MAC Relay Entity, of the Internal Sublayer Service provided by the individual MAC Entities associated with each Bridge Port is specified in 3.5 and 3.6.

Frames are accepted for transmission and delivered on reception to and from Processes and Entities that model the operation of the MAC Relay Entity in a Bridge. These are

(1) The Forwarding Process (3.7), which forwards received frames that are to be relayed to other Bridge Ports, filtering frames on the basis of information contained in the Filtering Database (3.9) and on the state of the Bridge Ports (3.4).

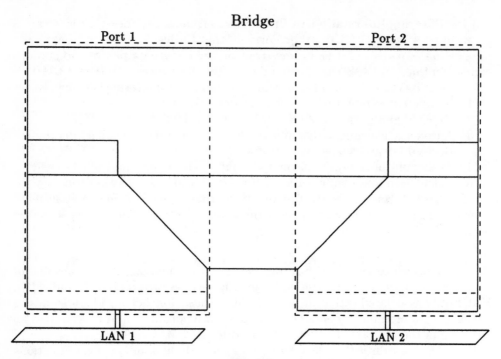

Fig 3-2
Bridge Ports

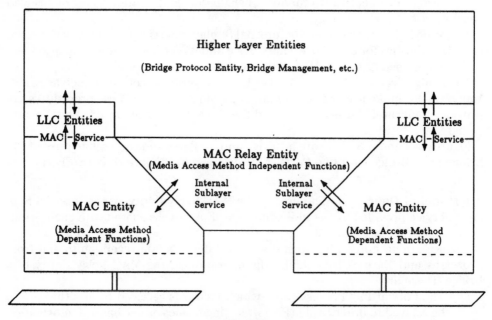

Fig 3-3
Bridge Architecture

(2) The Learning Process (3.8), which, by observing the source addresses of frames received on each Port, updates the Filtering Database (3.9) conditionally on the state of the Port (3.4) on which frames are observed.

(3) The Filtering Database (3.9), which holds filtering information either explicitly configured by management action or automatically entered by the Learning Process, and which supports queries by the Forwarding Process as to whether frames with given values of the destination MAC address field should be forwarded to a given Port.

Each Bridge Port also functions as an end station providing the MAC Service to LLC which supports

(1) The Bridge Protocol Entity (3.10), which operates a MAC Sublayer configuration protocol (Section 4) between Bridges, which determines, in part, the state of each Bridge Port (3.4) and its participation in the active topology of the Bridged Local Area Network.

(2) Other users of LLC, such as protocols providing Bridge Management (3.11).

Each Bridge Port shall support the operation of LLC Type 1 procedures in order to support the operation of the Bridge Protocol Entity. Bridge Ports may support other types of LLC procedures, which may be used by other protocols.

Figure 3-4 illustrates a single instance of frame relay between the Ports of a Bridge with two Ports.

Figure 3-5 illustrates the inclusion of information carried by a single frame, received on one of the Ports of a Bridge with two Ports, in the Filtering Database.

Figure 3-6 illustrates the reception and transmission of Bridge Protocol Data Units by the Bridge Protocol Entity.

Fig 3-4
Relaying MAC Frames

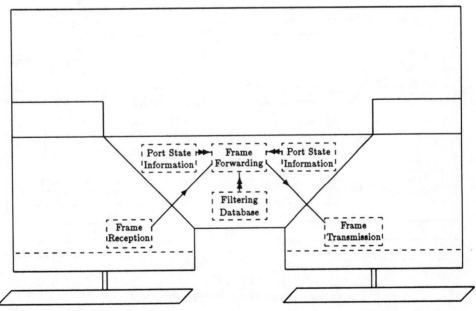

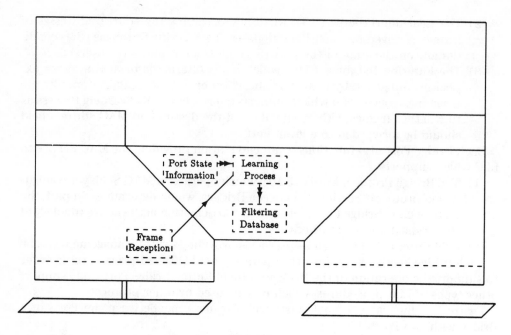

Fig 3-5
Observation of Network Traffic

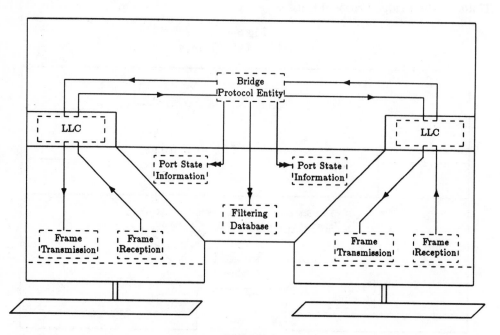

Fig 3-6
Operation of Inter-Bridge Protocol

3.4 Port State Information. State information associated with each Bridge Port governs its participation in the Bridged Local Area Network. If management permits a Port to participate in frame relay, and if it is capable of doing so, then it is described as active.

This standard specifies the use of a Spanning Tree Algorithm and Protocol which reduces the topology of the Bridged Local Area Network to a simply connected active topology (Section 4). Subsection 4.4 specifies the Port States associated with that mechanism. Ports that continue to participate in frame relay are described as being in a forwarding state.

The incorporation of end station location information in the Filtering Database by the Learning Process also depends on the active topology. If information associated with frames received on a Port is to be incorporated in the Filtering Database by the Learning Process, then the Port is described as being in a learning state; otherwise, it is in a non-learning state.

Figure 3-6 illustrates the operation of the Bridge Protocol Entity which operates the Spanning Tree Algorithm and Protocol, and its modification of Port state information as part of determining the active topology of the Bridged Local Area Network.

Figure 3-5 illustrates the use of the Port state information for a Port receiving a frame, by the Learning Process, in order to determine whether the station location information should be incorporated in the Filtering Database.

Figure 3-4 illustrates the use of the Port state information for a Port receiving a frame, by the Forwarding Process, in order to determine whether the received frame should be relayed through other Ports on the Bridge; and the use of the Port state information for a second Bridge Port in order to determine whether the relayed frame should be forwarded through that Port.

3.5 Frame Reception. The individual MAC Entity associated with each Bridge Port examines all frames transmitted on the LAN to which it is attached.

Frames that are in error as defined by the relevant media access method shall be discarded; this includes frames whose FCS is in error.

All other frames shall be submitted to the Learning Process.

Frames with M_UNITDATA.indication primitive frame_type and mac_action parameter values of user_data_frame and request_with_no_response, respectively (2.5), are submitted to the Forwarding Process. Frames with other values of frame_type and mac_action parameters, such as request_with_response and response frames, are discarded and shall not be relayed by the Bridge.

Frames addressed to the Bridge Port as an end station, with a frame_type of user_data_frame, shall be submitted to LLC. Such frames carry either the individual MAC Address of the Port or a group address associated with the Port (3.12) in the destination address field.

Frames relayed to a Bridge Port from other Bridge Ports in the same Bridge, and addressed to that Bridge Port as an end station, shall also be submitted to LLC.

3.6 Frame Transmission. The individual MAC Entity associated with each Bridge Port transmits frames submitted to it by the MAC Relay Entity.

Relayed frames are submitted for transmission by the Forwarding Process. The M_UNITDATA.request primitive associated with such frames conveys the values of the source and destination address fields received in the corresponding M_UNIT-DATA.indication primitive.

LLC Protocol Data Units are submitted by LLC as a user of the MAC Service provided by the Bridge Port. Frames transmitted to convey such Protocol Data Units carry the individual MAC Address of the Port in the source address field.

Each frame is transmitted subject to the MAC procedures to be observed for that specific IEEE 802 LAN technology. The values of the frame_type and mac_action parameters of the corresponding M_UNITDATA.request primitive shall be user_data_frame and request_with_no_response respectively (2.5).

Frames transmitted following a request by the LLC user of the MAC Service provided by the Bridge Port shall also be submitted to the MAC Relay Entity.

3.7 Frame Forwarding. The Forwarding Process forwards received frames that are to be relayed to other Bridge Ports, filtering frames on the basis of information contained in the Filtering Database and on the state of the Bridge Ports.

3.7.1 Forwarding Conditions. A frame received on a Bridge Port and submitted to the Forwarding Process shall be queued for transmission on each of the other Bridge Ports if, and only if

(1) The Port on which the frame was received was in a forwarding state (4.4), and

(2) The Port on which the frame is to be transmitted is in a forwarding state, and

(3) Either

  (a) The Filtering Database indicates that frames with this value of the destination MAC address field should be forwarded through the transmission Port (as would happen, for example, if the destination address was not in the database), or

  (b) The values of the source and destination MAC address fields are the same, and the Bridge is configured to not filter such frames, and

(4) The Maximum Service Data Unit Size supported by the LAN to which the transmission Port is attached would not be exceeded.

3.7.2 LLC Duplicate Address Check. A Bridge may either:

(1) Filter frames whose source and destination MAC address fields have the same value, in order to localize traffic, or

(2) Forward such frames, in order to support the optional LLC duplicate address check function.

3.7.3 Queued Frames. The Forwarding Process provides storage for queued frames, awaiting an opportunity to submit these for transmission to the individual MAC Entities associated with each Bridge Port. The order of queued frames shall be maintained.

A frame queued by the Forwarding Process for transmission on a Port shall be removed from that queue on submission to the individual MAC Entity for that Port;

no further attempt shall be made to transmit the frame on that Port even if the transmission is known to have failed.

A frame queued by the Forwarding Process for transmission on a Port can be removed from that queue, and not subsequently transmitted, if the time for which buffering is guaranteed has been exceeded for that frame.

A frame queued for transmission on a Port shall be removed from that queue, and not subsequently submitted to the individual MAC Entity for that Port, if that is necessary to ensure that the maximum bridge transit delay (2.3.6) will not be exceeded at the time at which the frame would be subsequently transmitted.

A frame queued for transmission on a Port shall be removed from that queue if the associated Port leaves the Forwarding state.

Removal of a frame from a queue for transmission on any particular Port does not of itself imply that it shall be removed from a queue for transmission on any other Port.

3.7.4 Priority Mapping. The Forwarding Process performs the mapping of the priority of forwarded frames (2.3.9). It determines the values of the user_priority and access_priority parameters used to relay frames.

The user_priority parameter in an M_UNITDATA.request primitive (2.5) shall be

(1) Equal to the value of the user_priority of the corresponding M_UNIT-DATA.indication primitive, if that was specified; i.e., if the frame was received from a LAN using the token-passing bus or token-passing ring access method, or

(2) Set to the value of the Outbound User Priority parameter (see below) for the transmission Port, if the value in the corresponding M_UNITDATA.indication primitive was unspecified; i.e., if the frame was received from a LAN using the CSMA/CD access method.

The access_priority parameter in an M_UNITDATA.request primitive (2.5) shall be either

(a) Set to the value of the Outbound Access Priority parameter (see below) for the transmission Port, or

(b) Equal to the value of the user_priority parameter in the request primitive.

The Outbound User Priority and Outbound Access Priority parameters may be set by management. If this capability is provided the value of the parameters shall be independently settable for each transmission Port, and the Bridge shall have the capability to use the full range of values in the parameter ranges specified in Tables 3-1 and 3-2. If this capability is not provided, the Bridge shall use the default values specified in Tables 3-1 and 3-2.

Note that the CSMA/CD access method treats all values of access_priority equally and does not signal user_priority. The Outbound User Priority and Outbound Access Priority parameters are still specified for this access method to allow a consistent approach to the management of Bridge Ports of different MAC types.

3.7.5 FCS Recalculation. Where a frame is being forwarded between two individual MAC Entities of the same IEEE 802 LAN type the FCS received in the M_UNITDATA.indication primitive may be supplied in the corresponding M_UNIT-DATA.request primitive and not recalculated (2.3.7).

39

Table 3-1
Outbound User Priorities

Parameter	Recommended or Default Value	Range
Outbound User Priority (ISO/IEC 8802-3 CSMA/CD)	0	0 – 7
Outbound User Priority (ISO/IEC 8802-4 Token Bus)	0	0 – 7
Outbound User Priority (IEEE Std 802.5 Token Ring)	0	0 – 7

Table 3-2
Outbound Access Priorities

Parameter	Recommended or Default Value	Range
Outbound Access Priority (ISO/IEC 8802-3 CSMA/CD)	0	0 – 7
Outbound Access Priority (ISO/IEC 8802-4 Token Bus)	0	0 – 7
Outbound Access Priority (IEEE Std 802.5 Token Ring)	4	0 – 7

Where the LANs are of different types this is not possible, and the FCS is recalculated according to the specific MAC procedures of the transmitting MAC Entity.

3.7.6 Model. Figure 3-4 illustrates the operation of the Forwarding Process in a single instance of frame relay between the Ports of a Bridge with two Ports.

3.8 The Learning Process. The Learning Process observes the source addresses of frames received on each Port and updates the Filtering Database conditionally on the state of the receiving Port.

Frames are submitted to the Learning Process by the individual MAC Entities associated with each Bridge Port as specified in 3.5.

The Learning Process may deduce the path through the Bridged Local Area Network to particular end stations by inspection of the source address field of received frames. It shall create or update a dynamic entry (3.9, 3.9.2) in the Filtering Database, associating the Port on which the frame was received with the MAC address in the source address field of the frame, if and only if

(1) The Port on which the frame was received is in a state that allows learning (4.4), and
(2) The source address field of the frame denotes a specific end station, i.e., is not a group address, and
(3) A static entry (3.9, 3.9.1) for the associated MAC address does not already exist, and
(4) The resulting number of entries would not exceed the capacity of the Filtering Database.

If the Filtering Database is already filled up to its capacity, but a new entry would otherwise be made, then an existing entry may be removed to make room for the new entry.

Figure 3-5 illustrates the operation of the Learning Process in the inclusion of station location information carried by a single frame, received on one of the Ports of a Bridge, in the Filtering Database.

3.9 The Filtering Database. The Filtering Database holds filtering information that is either explicitly configured by management action or automatically entered by the Learning Process. It supports queries by the Forwarding Process as to whether frames with given values of the destination MAC address field should be forwarded to a given Port.

The Filtering Database shall contain static entries (3.9.1). It shall be capable of containing dynamic entries (3.9.2). Both types of entry shall not exist for a given MAC address: a dynamic entry shall not be created if a static entry for the same MAC address already exists; creation of a static entry shall cause the removal of a dynamic entry for the same address if one exists.

The Filtering Database may be interrogated and updated by management. Such management may be carried out by local or private means, or by use of the remote management capability provided by Bridge Management (3.11) using the operations specified in Section 6.

3.9.1 Static Entries. Static entries may be added to and removed from the Filtering Database under explicit management control. They are not automatically removed by any timeout mechanism.

Static entries specify

(1) The MAC address for which filtering is specified.
(2) For each inbound Port on which frames are received, a Port map that specifies for each outbound Port on which frames may be transmitted, whether frames shall be filtered or forwarded to that Port.

The MAC addresses that can be specified shall include group addresses and the broadcast address.

3.9.2 Dynamic Entries. Dynamic entries are created and updated by the Learning Process as described in 3.8. They shall be automatically removed after a specified time has elapsed since the entry was created or last updated. This timing out of entries ensures that end stations that have been moved to a different part of the Bridged Local Area Network will not be permanently prevented from receiving frames. It also takes account of changes in the active topology of the Bridged Local Area Network which can cause end stations to appear to move from the point of view of a Bridge; i.e., the path to those end stations subsequently lies through a different Bridge Port.

The timeout value, or Ageing Time, after which a dynamic entry is automatically removed, may be set by management (Section 6). A recommended default value for use in IEEE 802 Bridged Local Area Networks is specified in Table 3-3; this is suggested in order to remove the need for explicit setting of the value in most cases. Table 3-3 also specifies a range of applicable values. If the value of Ageing Time can be set by management, the Bridge shall have the capability to use values in the range specified, with a granularity of 1 second.

The Spanning Tree Algorithm and Protocol specified in Section 4 includes a procedure for notifying all Bridges in the Bridged Local Area Network of topology changes and specifies a short value for the timeout value which is enforced for a period after any topology change. This procedure allows the normal timeout, operable during periods in which the topology does not change, to be long enough to cope with periods for which addressed end stations do not generate frames themselves, perhaps through being powered down, while not sacrificing the ability of the Bridged Local Area Network to continue to provide a service after automatic reconfiguration.

Dynamic entries specify

(1) The MAC address for which filtering is specified.

(2) A Port number.

Frames with the specified destination MAC address shall be forwarded only to the specified Port. A dynamic entry acts like a static entry with a single Port selected in the Port map.

The MAC addresses specified in dynamic entries shall not include group addresses and the broadcast address.

3.9.3 Permanent Database. The Filtering Database contains a Permanent Database which provides fixed storage for static entries. The Filtering Database shall be initialized with the static entries contained in this fixed data store.

Static entries may be added to and removed from the Permanent Database under explicit management control.

3.9.4 Model of Operation. Figure 3-6 illustrates the operation of the Bridge Protocol Entity (3.10), which operates the Spanning Tree Algorithm and Protocol, and its notification of the Filtering Database of changes in active topology signalled by that protocol.

Table 3-3
Ageing Time Parameter Value

Parameter	Recommended Default Value	Range	
Ageing Time	300.0	10.0 –	1.0×10^6

All times are in seconds.

Figure 3-5 illustrates the creation or update of a dynamic entry in the Filtering Database by the Learning Process.

Figure 3-4 illustrates the use of the Filtering Database by the Forwarding Process in a single instance of frame relay between the Ports of a Bridge with two Ports.

3.10 Bridge Protocol Entity. The Bridge Protocol Entity operates the Spanning Tree Algorithm and Protocol.

The Bridge Protocol Entities of Bridges attached, through their Ports, to the same individual LANs in a Bridged Local Area Network, communicate by exchanging Bridge Protocol Data Units (BPDUs).

Figure 3-6 illustrates the operation of the Bridge Protocol Entity including the reception and transmission of frames containing BPDUs, the modification of the state information associated with individual Bridge Ports, and notification of the Filtering Database of changes in active topology.

3.11 Bridge Management. Remote management facilities may be provided by the Bridge.

The facilities provided and the operations that support these are specified in Section 6.

Section 7 specifies the protocol operations, identifiers, and values to be used in realizing these management operations through the use of P802.1B [3].

Bridge Management protocols use the Service provided by the operation of LLC Procedures, which use the MAC Service provided by the Bridged Local Area Network.

3.12 Addressing. All MAC Entities communicating across a Bridged Local Area Network shall use the same length of MAC address, i.e. either all stations use 16-bit addresses or all stations use 48-bit addresses.

A Bridge may use

(1) 48-bit Universally Administered Addresses, or
(2) 48-bit Locally Administered Addresses, or
(3) 16-bit Locally Administered Addresses.

The specific MAC address used by every MAC Entity communicating across the Bridged Local Area Network shall be unique in that network in order to specify the addressed station unambiguously.

3.12.1 End Stations. Frames transmitted between end stations using the MAC Service provided by a Bridged Local Area Network carry the MAC address of the source and destination peer end stations in the source and destination address fields of the frames, respectively. The address, or other means of identification, of a Bridge is not carried in frames transmitted between peer users for the purpose of frame relay in the Bridged Local Area Network.

The broadcast address and other group addresses apply to the use of the MAC Service provided by the Bridged Local Area Network as a whole. Frames with such values of the destination address field are, in the absence of explicit management configuration of the Filtering Database (3.9, Section 6), relayed throughout the Bridged Local Area Network.

3.12.2 Bridge Ports. The individual MAC Entity associated with each Bridge Port shall have a separate specific MAC Address. This address is used by the MAC procedures operated by the MAC Entity, if required by the particular Media Access Method employed.

Frames that are received from the LAN to which a Port is attached and which carry a MAC address for the Port in the destination address field are submitted to the MAC Service User (LLC) exactly as for an end station.

3.12.3 Bridge Protocol Entities. Bridge Protocol Entities only receive and transmit BPDUs. These are only received and transmitted from other Bridge Protocol Entities (or in circumstances where two Bridge Ports are connected to the same LAN, to and from themselves).

A Bridge Protocol Entity uses the DL_UNITDATA.request primitive provided by the individual LLC Entities associated with each active Bridge Port to transmit BPDUs. Each BPDU is transmitted on one selected Bridge Port. BPDUs are received through corresponding DL_UNITDATA.indication primitives. The source_address and destination_address parameters of the DL_UNITDATA.request primitive shall both denote the Standard LSAP assigned to the Bridge Spanning Tree Protocol. This identifies the Bridge Protocol Entity among other users of LLC.

Each DL_UNITDATA.request primitive gives rise to the transmission of an LLC UI command PDU which conveys the BPDU in its information field. The source and destination LSAP address fields are set to the values supplied in the request primitive.

The value assigned to the Bridge Spanning Tree Protocol LSAP is given in Table 3-5. The full list of standard LSAP assignments and criteria for assignment can be obtained on request from the IEEE Standards Office, 345 East 47th Street, New York, NY 10017-2394.

This standard defines a Protocol Identifier field, present in all BPDUs (Section 5), which serves to identify different protocols supported by Bridge Protocol Entities, within the scope of the LSAP Assignment. This standard specifies a single value of the Protocol Identifier in Section 5. This value serves to identify BPDUs exchanged between Bridge Protocol Entities operating the Spanning Tree Algorithm and Protocol specified in Section 4. Further values of this field are reserved for future standardization.

A Bridge Protocol Entity that receives a BPDU with an unknown Protocol Identifier shall discard that BPDU.

A Bridge Protocol Entity that operates the Spanning Tree Algorithm and Protocol specified in Section 4 of this standard always transmits BPDUs addressed to all other Bridge Protocol Entities attached to the LAN on which the frame containing the BPDU was transmitted. A group address shall be used in the destination address field to address this group of Entities. This group address shall be configured in the Permanent Database (3.12.6) in order to confine BPDUs to the individual LAN on which they are transmitted.

A 48-bit Universal Address, known as the Bridge Group Address, has been assigned for this purpose. Its value is specified in Table 3-2. Bridges that use 48-bit Universally Administered Addresses shall use this address in the destination address field of all MAC frames conveying BPDUs.

The source address field of MAC frames conveying BPDUs contains the specific MAC Address for the Bridge Port through which the BPDU is transmitted (3.12.2).

3.12.4 Bridge Management Entities. Bridge Management Entities transmit and receive protocol data units using the Service provided by the individual LLC Entities associated with each Bridge Port. Each of these in turn uses the MAC Service, which is provided by the individual MAC Entities associated with that Port and supported by the Bridged Local Area Network as a whole.

As a user of the MAC Service provided by a Bridged Local Area Network, the Bridge Management Entity may be attached to any point in the Bridged Local Area Network. Frames addressed to the Bridge Management Entity will be relayed by Bridges if necessary to reach the LAN to which it is attached.

In order to ensure that received frames are not duplicated, the basic requirement in a single LAN or a Bridged Local Area Network that a unique address be associated with each point of attachment shall be met.

A Bridge Management Entity for a specific Bridge is addressed by one or more specific MAC addresses in conjunction with the higher layer protocol identifier and addressing information. It may share one or more points of attachment to the Bridged Local Area Network with the Ports of the Bridge with which it is associated. It is recommended that it make use of the MAC Service provided by all the MAC Entities associated with each Bridge Port, i.e., that it be reachable through each Bridge Port using frames carrying the specific MAC address of that Port in the destination address field.

This Standard specifies a standard group address for public use which serves to convey management requests to the Bridge Management Entities associated with all Bridge Ports attached to a Bridged Local Area Network. A management request that is conveyed in a MAC frame carrying this address value in the destination address field will generally elicit multiple responses from a single Bridge. This address is known as the All LANs Bridge Management Group Address and takes the value specified in Table 3-5.

3.12.5 Unique Identification of a Bridge. It is necessary for the operation of the Bridge Protocol specified in Section 4, that a single unique identifier be associated with each Bridge. This identifier is derived from a unique MAC address for the Bridge, known as the Bridge Address.

In a Bridged Local Area Network utilizing locally assigned 16-bit addresses, this address shall be unique among all those assigned in the Bridged Local Area Network.

In a Bridged Local Area Network utilizing 48-bit addresses, this address shall be assigned to be globally unique, i.e., it shall be a 48-bit Universally Administered Address.

It is recommended that this address be the specific MAC Address of the lowest numbered Bridge Port (Port 1).

The unique Bridge Identifier used by the Spanning Tree Algorithm and Protocol is derived from the Bridge Address, as specified in 4.5.3 and 5.2.5.

3.12.6 Reserved Addresses. Frames containing any of the group addresses specified in Table 3-4 in their destination address field shall not be relayed by the Bridge. They shall be configured in the Permanent Database. Management shall not

Table 3-4
Reserved Addresses

Assignment	Value
Bridge Group Address	01-80-C2-00-00-00
Reserved for future standardization	01-80-C2-00-00-01
Reserved for future standardization	01-80-C2-00-00-02
Reserved for future standardization	01-80-C2-00-00-03
Reserved for future standardization	01-80-C2-00-00-04
Reserved for future standardization	01-80-C2-00-00-05
Reserved for future standardization	01-80-C2-00-00-06
Reserved for future standardization	01-80-C2-00-00-07
Reserved for future standardization	01-80-C2-00-00-08
Reserved for future standardization	01-80-C2-00-00-09
Reserved for future standardization	01-80-C2-00-00-0A
Reserved for future standardization	01-80-C2-00-00-0B
Reserved for future standardization	01-80-C2-00-00-0C
Reserved for future standardization	01-80-C2-00-00-0D
Reserved for future standardization	01-80-C2-00-00-0E
Reserved for future standardization	01-80-C2-00-00-0F

Table 3-5
Addressing Bridge Management

Assignment	Value
All LANs Bridge Management Group Address	01-80-C2-00-00-10

provide the capability to remove these addresses from the Permanent or the Filtering Databases. These group addresses are reserved for assignment to standard protocols, according to the criteria for such assignments (IEEE Std 802 [2], 5.5).

Other group addresses may be configured as static entries in the Permanent Database, without the need for explicit initialization through management. Management may provide the capability to remove these addresses from the Permanent or Filtering Database.

Table 3-6 records values of functional addresses specified in IEEE Std 802.5 [7] that are used in the destination address field of MAC frames that can have frame_ type and mac_action parameter values of user_data_frame and request_with_no_ response, respectively, but should not be relayed from the token ring on which they are initially transmitted.

Table 3-6
Functional Addresses as Specified in IEEE Std 802.5 [7]

Assignment	Value (16-bit)	Value (48-bit)
Bridge Functional Address	01-04	03-00-00-00-80-00

Table 3-7
Standard LSAP Assignment

Assignment	Value
Bridge Spanning Tree Protocol	01000010

Code Representation: The least significant bit of the value shown is the left-most. The bits increase in significance from left to right.

4. The Spanning Tree Algorithm and Protocol

The configuration algorithm and protocol described in this section reduce the Bridged Local Area Network topology to a single Spanning Tree.

4.1 Requirements to be Met by the Algorithm. The Spanning Tree Algorithm and its associated Bridge Protocol operate to Support, Preserve, and Maintain the Quality of the MAC Service in all its aspects as discussed in Section 2. In order to perform this function, the algorithm meets the following requirements, each of which is related to the discussion in that section:

(1) It will configure the active topology of a Bridged Local Area Network of arbitrary topology into a single spanning tree, such that there is at most one data route between any two end stations, eliminating data loops (2.3.3; 2.3.4).

(2) It will provide for fault tolerance by automatic reconfiguration of the spanning tree topology as a result of Bridge failure or a breakdown in a data path, within the confines of the available Bridged Local Area Network components, and for the automatic accommodation of any Bridge or Bridge Port added to the Bridged Local Area Network without the formation of transient data loops (2.1).

(3) The entire active topology will stabilize in any sized Bridged Local Area Network. It will, with a high probability, stabilize within a short, known bounded interval in order to minimize the time for which the service is unavailable for communication between any pair of end stations (2.1).

(4) The active topology will be predictable and reproducible, and may be selected by management of the parameters of the algorithm, thus allowing the application of Configuration Management, following traffic analysis, to meet the goals of Performance Management (2.1; 2.3.10).

(5) It will operate transparently to the end stations, such that they are unaware of their attachment to a single LAN or a Bridged Local Area Network when using the MAC Service (2.2).

(6) The communications bandwidth consumed by the Bridges in establishing and maintaining the spanning tree on any particular LAN will be a small percentage of the total available bandwidth and independent of the total traffic supported by the Bridged Local Area Network regardless of the total number of Bridges or LANs (2.3.10).

Additionally, the algorithm and protocol meet the following goals which limit the complexity of Bridges and their configuration:

(a) The memory requirements associated with each Bridge Port are independent of the number of Bridges and LANs in the Bridged Local Area Network.

(b) Bridges do not have to be individually configured before being added to the Bridged Local Area Network, other than having their MAC addresses assigned through normal procedures.

4.2 Requirements of the MAC Bridges. In order for the Bridge Protocol to operate, the following are required:

(1) A unique MAC group address, recognized by all the Bridges within the Bridged Local Area Network, that identifies the Bridge Protocol Entities of all Bridges attached to an individual LAN.

(2) An identifier for each Bridge, unique within the Bridged Local Area Network.

(3) A distinct Port identifier for each Bridge Port, that can be assigned independently of the values used in other Bridges.

Values for each of these parameters, or a mechanism for assigning values to them, shall be provided by each Bridge. In the case of MAC Bridges that use 48-bit Universally Administered Addresses, the unique MAC Address that identifies the Bridge Protocol Entities is the Bridge Group Address (3.12.3).

In addition, to allow the configuration of the Spanning Tree active topology to be managed, the following are required:

(a) A means of assigning the relative priority of each Bridge within the set of Bridges in the Bridged Local Area Network.

(b) A means of assigning the relative priority of each Port within the set of Ports of an individual Bridge.

(c) A means of assigning a path cost component to each Port.

These parameters may be set by management.

The unique identifier for each Bridge is derived, in part, from the Bridge Address (3.12.5) and, in part, from a manageable priority component (5.2.5). The relative priority of Bridges is determined by the numerical comparison of the unique identifiers, with the lower numerical value indicating the higher priority identifier.

Part of the identifier for each Port is fixed and is different for each Port on a Bridge, and part is a manageable priority component (5.2.7). The relative priority of Ports is determined by the numerical comparison of the unique identifiers, with the lower numerical value indicating the higher priority identifier.

The path cost associated with each Port may be manageable. Additionally, 4.10.2 recommends default values for Ports attached to LANs of specific MAC types and speeds.

4.3 Overview

4.3.1 The Active Topology and Its Computation. The Spanning Tree Algorithm and Protocol configure a simply connected active topology from the arbitrarily connected components of a Bridged Local Area Network. Frames are forwarded through some of the Bridge Ports in the Bridged Local Area Network and not through others, which are held in a blocking state. At any time, Bridges effectively connect just the LANs to which Ports in a forwarding state are attached. Frames are forwarded in both directions through Bridge Ports that are in a forwarding state. Ports that are in a blocking state do not forward frames in either direction but may be included in the active topology, i.e., be put into a forwarding state if components fail, are removed, or are added.

Figure 2-2 shows an example of a Bridged Local Area Network. Figure 4-1 shows the active topology, i.e., the logical connectivity, of the same Bridged Local Area Network following configuration.

One of the Bridges is known as the Root or the Root Bridge in the Bridged Local Area Network. Each individual LAN has a Bridge Port connected to it that forwards frames from that LAN towards the Root and forwards frames from the direction of the Root onto that LAN. This Port is known as the Designated Port for that LAN, and the Bridge of which it is part is the Designated Bridge for the LAN. The Root is the Designated Bridge for all the LANs to which it is connected. The Ports on each Bridge that are in a forwarding state are the Root Port (that closest to the Root — see below) and the Designated Ports (if there are any).

In Fig 4-1, Bridge 1 has been selected as the Root (though one cannot tell simply by looking at the topology which Bridge is the Root) and is the Designated Bridge for LAN 1 and LAN 2. Bridge 2 is the Designated Bridge for LAN 3 and LAN 4, and Bridge 4 is the Designated Bridge for LAN 5. Figure 4-2 shows the logical tree topology of this configuration of the Bridged Local Area Network.

The stable active topology of a Bridged Local Area Network is determined by

(1) The unique Bridge Identifiers associated with each Bridge.
(2) The Path Cost associated with each Bridge Port.
(3) The Port Identifier associated with each Bridge Port

The Bridge with the highest priority Bridge Identifier is the Root (for convenience of calculation this is the identifier with the lowest numerical value). Every Bridge Port in the Bridged Local Area Network has a Root Path Cost associated with it. This is the sum of the Path Costs for each Bridge Port receiving frames forwarded from the Root on the least cost path to the Bridge. The Designated Port for each LAN is the Bridge Port for which the value of the Root Path Cost is the lowest: if two or more Ports have the same value of Root Path Cost, then first the Bridge Identifier of their Bridges and then their Port Identifiers are used as tie-breakers. Thus, a single Bridge Port is selected as the Designated Port for each LAN, the same computation selects the Root Port of a Bridge from amongst the Bridge's own Ports, and the active topology of the Bridged Local Area Network is completely determined.

A component of the Bridge Identifier of each Bridge, and the Path Cost and Port Identifier of each Bridge Port, can be managed, thus allowing a manager to select the active topology of the Bridged Local Area Network.

4.3.2 Propagating the Topology Information. Bridges send a type of Bridge Protocol Data Unit known as a Configuration BPDU to each other in order to communicate and compute the above information. A MAC frame conveying a BPDU carries the Bridge Group Address in the destination address field and is received by all the Bridges connected to the LAN on which the frame is transmitted.

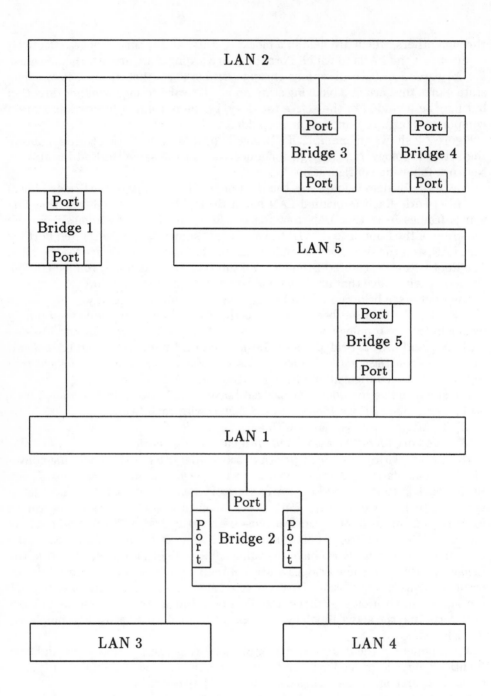

Fig 4-1
Active Topology

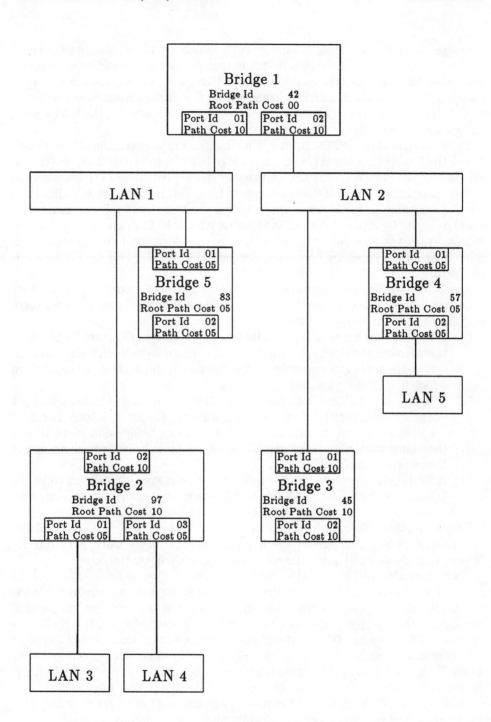

Fig 4-2
Spanning Tree

Bridge Protocol Data Units are not directly forwarded by Bridges, but the information in them may be used by a Bridge in calculating its own BPDU to transmit, and may stimulate that transmission. The Configuration BPDU, which is conveyed between the Bridge Ports attached to a single LAN, is distinguished from the notion of a Configuration Message, which expresses the propagation of the information carried throughout the Bridged Local Area Network.

Each Configuration BPDU contains, among other parameters, the unique identifier of the Bridge that the transmitting Bridge believes to be the Root, the cost of the path to the Root from the transmitting Port, the identifier of the transmitting Bridge, and the identifier of the transmitting Port. This information is sufficient to allow a receiving Bridge to determine whether the transmitting Port has a better claim to be the Designated Port on the LAN on which the Configuration BPDU was received than the Port currently believed to be the Designated Port, and to determine whether the receiving Port should become the Root Port for the Bridge if it is not already.

Timely propagation throughout the Bridged Local Area Network of the necessary information to allow all Bridge Ports to determine their state (blocking or forwarding) is achieved through three basic mechanisms:

(1) A Bridge that believes itself to be the Root (all Bridges start by believing themselves to be the Root until they discover otherwise); originates Configuration Messages (by transmitting Configuration BPDUs) on all the LANs to which it is attached, at regular intervals.

(2) A Bridge that receives a Configuration BPDU on what it decides is its Root Port conveying better information (i.e., highest priority Root Identifier, lowest Root Path Cost, highest priority transmitting Bridge and Port), passes that information on to all the LANs for which it believes itself to be the Designated Port.

(3) A Bridge that receives inferior information on a Port it considers to be the Designated Port on the LAN to which it is attached, transmits its own information in reply for all other Bridges attached to that LAN to hear.

Hence, Spanning Tree paths to the Bridge with highest priority Root Identifier are quickly learned throughout the Bridged Local Area Network, with inferior information about other potential roots and paths being contradicted.

4.3.3 Reconfiguration. To allow for reconfiguration of the Bridged Local Area Network when components are removed or when management changes are made to parameters determining the topology, the topology information propagated throughout the Bridged Local Area Network has a limited lifetime. This is effected by transmitting the age of the information conveyed (the time elapsed since the Configuration Message originated from the Root) in each Configuration BPDU. Every Bridge stores the information from the Designated Port on each of the LANs to which its Ports are connected, and monitors the age of that information.

In normal stable operation, the regular transmission of Configuration Messages by the Root ensures that topology information is not timed out.

If the Bridge times out the information held for a Port, it will attempt to become the Designated Port for the LAN to which that Port is attached, and will transmit protocol information received from the Root on its Root Port on to that LAN.

If the Root Port of the Bridge is timed out, then another Port may be selected as the Root Port. The information transmitted on LANs for which the Bridge is the Designated Bridge will then be calculated on the basis of information received on the new Root Port.

If no record of information from the current Root remains, then the Bridge will reconfigure by claiming to be the Root itself. If the Root has indeed failed, other Bridges will also be timing out protocol information; information as to the best successor and the new topology will rapidly propagate throughout the Bridged Local Area Network. It is also possible that the path to the current Root has changed, perhaps by increasing in cost, and that the reconfiguring Bridge has timed out because it considered more recent information from the Root inferior since it had a higher Root Path Cost. In this latter case, neighboring Bridges will immediately reply to BPDUs transmitted by the aspiring Root.

To ensure that all Bridges in the Bridged Local Area Network share a common understanding of when old information should be timed out, the timeout value is transmitted in all Configuration Messages from the Root. This value takes account of the propagation delays in transmitting and receiving BPDUs on each of the LANs in the Bridged Local Area Network, and thus of propagation of protocol information down the Spanning Tree. To minimize the probability of triggering reconfiguration through the loss of Configuration Messages, it includes an additional multiple of the time interval at which these are transmitted by the Root.

4.3.4 Changing Port State. Since there are propagation delays in passing protocol information throughout a Bridged Local Area Network, there cannot be a sharp transition from one active topology to another. Topology changes may take place at different times in different parts of the Bridged Local Area Network and to move a Bridge Port directly from non-participation in the active topology to the forwarding state would be to risk having temporary data loops and the duplication and misordering of frames. It is also desirable to allow other Bridges time to reply to inferior protocol information before starting to forward frames.

Bridge Ports must therefore wait for new topology information to propagate throughout the Bridged Local Area Network, and for the frame lifetime of any frames forwarded using the old active topology to expire, before forwarding frames.

During this time it is also desirable to time out station location information in the Filtering Database that may no longer be true and, during the latter part of this interval, to learn new station location information in order to minimize the effect of initial flooding of frames when the Port enters a forwarding state. When the algorithm decides that a Port should be put into the Forwarding State, it is, therefore, first put into a Listening State where it waits for protocol information that suggests it should return to the Blocking State, and for the expiry of a protocol timer that would move it into a Learning State. In the Learning State, it still blocks the forwarding of frames, but learned station location information is included by the Learning Process in the Filtering Database. Finally the expiry of a protocol timer moves it into the Forwarding State where both forwarding of relayed frames and learning of station location information are enabled.

Figure 4-3 shows the transitions between the Port States.

4.3.5 Notifying Topology Changes. In normal stable operation, station location information in the Filtering Database need only change as a consequence of the physical relocation of stations. It may, therefore, be desirable to employ a long ageing time for entries in the Filtering Database, especially as many end stations transmit frames following power-up after relocation which would cause station location information to be relearned.

However, when the active topology of a Bridged Local Area Network reconfigures, end stations may appear to move from the point of view of a Bridge in the network. This is true even if the states of the Ports on that Bridge have not changed. It is necessary for station location to be relearned following a change in the active topology, even if only part of the Bridged Local Area Network has reconfigured.

Fig 4-3
Port States

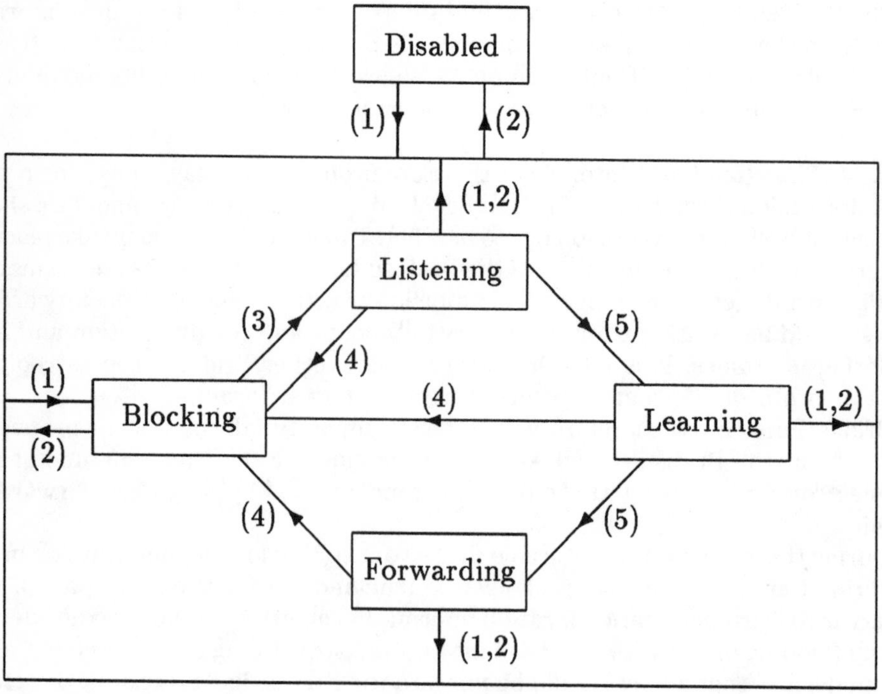

(1) Port enabled, by management or initialization
(2) Port disabled, by management or failure
(3) Algorithm selects as Designated or Root Port
(4) Algorithm selects as not Designated or Root Port
(5) Protocol timer expiry (Forwarding Timer)

The Spanning Tree Algorithm and Protocol provide procedures for a Bridge which detects a change in active topology to notify the Root of the change reliably, and for the Root subsequently to communicate the change to all the Bridges. The Bridges then use a short value to ageout dynamic entries in the Fitering Database for a period.

When a Bridge that is not the Root changes the active topology of the Bridged Local Area Network, it transmits a Topology Change Notification BPDU on the LAN to which its Root Port is attached. This transmission is repeated until the Bridge receives an acknowledgment from the Designated Bridge for that LAN. The acknowledgment is carried in a Configuration BPDU, thus the notification will eventually be acknowledged or further reconfiguration will take place. The Designated Bridge passes the notification to, or towards, the Root using the same procedure.

If the Root receives such a notification, or changes the topology itself, it will set a Topology Change flag in all Configuration Messages transmitted for some time. This time is such that all Bridges will receive one or more of the Configuration Messages, or further reconfiguration will take place. While this flag is set, Bridges use the value of Forwarding Delay (the time interval spent in each of the Listening and Learning States) to age out dynamic entries. When the flag is reset again, Bridges revert to using the Filtering Database Ageing Time.

4.4 Port States. The operation of an individual Bridge Port is described in terms of the State of the Port and the Processes (3.3) that provide and support the functions necessary for the operation of the Bridge (3.1).

The State of each Port governs the processing of frames received from the individual MAC Entity associated with the Port (3.5), the submission of frames to the MAC Entity for transmission (3.6), and the possible inclusion of the Port in the active topology of the Bridged Local Area Network.

The operation of the Spanning Tree Algorithm and Protocol serves to maintain and change the State of each Port in order to meet the requirements placed on the algorithm (4.1). The possible Port States and the associated rules relating to the processing of frames are particular to this algorithm and Bridge Protocol.

The following are specified below for each of the five States — Blocking, Listening, Learning, Forwarding, or Disabled — that a Port may be in:

(1) The purpose of the State.
(2) Whether the Forwarding Process (3.7) discards received frames.
(3) Whether the Forwarding Process (3.7) submits forwarded frames for transmission.
(4) How the Learning Process (3.8) processes received frames.
(5) Whether the Bridge Protocol Entity (3.10) includes the Port in its computation of the active topology.
(6) Under which conditions a Port enters and leaves the State.

4.4.1 Blocking. A Port in this State does not participate in frame relay, thus preventing frame duplication arising through multiple paths existing in the active topology of the Bridged Local Area Network.

The Forwarding Process shall discard received frames. It shall not submit forwarded frames for transmission. The Learning Process shall not add station location information to the Filtering Database.

The Bridge Protocol Entity shall include the Port in its computation of the active topology. BPDUs received shall be processed as required by the Spanning Tree Algorithm and Protocol.

This State is entered following initialization of the Bridge or from the Disabled State when the Port is enabled through the operation of management. This State may be entered from the Listening, Learning, or Forwarding States through the operation of the Spanning Tree Algorithm and Protocol. A Port enters the Blocking State because it has received information that another Bridge is the Designated Bridge for the LAN to which the Port is attached.

This State may be left upon expiry of a protocol timer or receipt of a Configuration BPDU on this or another Port, and the Listening State entered, through the operation of the Spanning Tree Algorithm and Protocol. This State may be left, and the Disabled State entered, through management action.

4.4.2 Listening. A Port in this State is preparing to participate in frame relay. Frame relay is temporarily disabled in order to prevent temporary loops, which may occur in a Bridged Local Area Network during the lifetime of this State as the active topology of the Bridged Local Area Network changes. Learning is disabled since changes in active topology may lead to the information acquired being incorrect when the active topology becomes stable.

The Forwarding Process shall discard received frames. It shall not submit forwarded frames for transmission. The Learning Process shall not add station location information to the Filtering Database.

The Bridge Protocol Entity shall include the Port in its computation of the active topology. BPDUs received shall be processed as required by the Spanning Tree Algorithm and Protocol. BPDUs can be submitted for transmission.

This State is entered from the Blocking State when the operation of the Spanning Tree Algorithm and Protocol determines that the Port should participate in frame relay.

This State may be left upon the expiry of a protocol timer, and the Learning State entered, through the operation of the Spanning Tree Algorithm and Protocol. This State may be left upon receipt of a Bridge Protocol Data Unit on this or another Port, and the Blocking State entered, through the operation of the Spanning Tree Algorithm and Protocol. This State may be left, and the Disabled or the Blocking State entered, through management action.

4.4.3 Learning. A Port in this State is preparing to participate in frame relay. Frame relay is temporarily disabled in order to prevent temporary loops, which may occur in a Bridged Local Area Network during the lifetime of this State as the active topology of the Bridged Local Area Network changes. Learning is enabled to allow information to be acquired prior to frame relay in order to reduce the number of frames unnecessarily relayed.

The Forwarding Process shall discard received frames. It shall not submit forwarded frames for transmission. The Learning Process shall incorporate station location information into the Filtering Database.

The Bridge Protocol Entity shall include the Port in its computation of the active topology. BPDUs received shall be processed as required by the Spanning Tree Algorithm and Protocol. BPDUs can be submitted for transmission.

This State is entered from the Listening State through the operation of the Spanning Tree Algorithm and Protocol, on the expiry of a protocol timer.

This State may be left upon the expiry of a protocol timer, and the Forwarding State entered, through the operation of the Spanning Tree Algorithm and Protocol. This State may be left upon receipt of a Bridge Protocol Data Unit on this or another Port, and the Blocking State entered, through the operation of the Spanning Tree Algorithm and Protocol. This State may be left, and the Disabled or the Blocking State entered, through management action.

4.4.4 Forwarding. A Port in this State is participating in frame relay.

The Forwarding Process can forward received frames. It can submit forwarded frames for transmission. The Learning Process shall incorporate station location information into the Filtering Database.

The Bridge Protocol Entity shall include the Port in its computation of the active topology. BPDUs received shall be processed as required by the Spanning Tree Algorithm and Protocol. BPDUs can be submitted for transmission.

This State is entered from the Learning State through the operation of the Spanning Tree Algorithm and Protocol, on the expiry of a protocol timer.

This State may be left upon receipt of a Bridge Protocol Data Unit on this or another Port, and the Blocking State entered, through the operation of the Spanning Tree Algorithm and Protocol. This State may be left, and the Disabled or the Blocking State entered, through management action.

4.4.5 Disabled. A Port in this State does not participate in frame relay or the operation of the Spanning Tree Algorithm and Protocol.

The Forwarding Process shall discard received frames. It shall not submit forwarded frames for transmission. The Learning Process shall not incorporate station location information into the Filtering Database.

The Bridge Protocol Entity shall not include the Port in its computation of the active topology. BPDUs received shall not be processed by the Spanning Tree Algorithm and Protocol. BPDUs shall not be submitted for transmission.

This State is entered from any other State by the operation of management.

This State is left when the Port is enabled by management action, and the Blocking State is entered.

4.5 Protocol Parameters and Timers. Information is transferred between the Protocol Entities of individual Bridges by the exchange of Bridge Protocol Data Units. This section specifies the parameters conveyed in the two types of BPDU specified: Configuration BPDUs and Topology Change Notification BPDUs. The encoding of these parameters and additional information elements are specified in Section 5.

Each Bridge Protocol Entity maintains a number of parameters and timers independently of the individual Ports, and a number of timers and parameters for each Port. This section specifies those parameters, their use, and under what conditions they are updated.

4.5.1 Configuration BPDU Parameters

4.5.1.1 Root Identifier. The unique Bridge Identifier of the Bridge assumed to be the Root by the Bridge transmitting the Configuration BPDU.

This parameter is conveyed to enable all Bridges to agree on the Root.

4.5.1.2 Root Path Cost. The Cost of the path to the Root Bridge denoted by the Root Identifier from the transmitting Bridge.

This parameter is conveyed to enable a Bridge to decide which of the Bridges attached to the LAN on which the Configuration BPDU has been received offers the lowest Cost path to the Root for that LAN.

4.5.1.3 Bridge Identifier. The unique Bridge Identifier of the Bridge transmitting the Configuration BPDU.

This parameter is conveyed to enable a Bridge to

(1) Decide, in the case of a LAN to which two or more Bridges are attached, which offer equal Cost paths to the Root, which of the Bridges should be selected as the Designated Bridge for that LAN.

(2) Detect the case where two or more Ports on the same Bridge are attached to the same LAN, i.e., are in direct communication through a path of Bridged Local Area Network components none of which operate the Spanning Tree Algorithm and Protocol.

4.5.1.4 Port Identifier. The Port Identifier of the Port on the transmitting Bridge through which the Configuration BPDU was transmitted. This identifier uniquely identifies a Port on that Bridge.

This parameter is conveyed to enable a Bridge to decide, in the case of a LAN to which two or more Ports on the same Bridge are attached, which Ports are so attached.

4.5.1.5 Message Age. The age of the Configuration Message, being the time since the generation of the Configuration BPDU by the Root that instigated the generation of this Configuration BPDU.

This parameter is conveyed to enable a Bridge to discard information whose age exceeds Max Age (see below).

4.5.1.6 Max Age. A timeout value to be used by all Bridges in the Bridged Local Area Network. The value of Max Age is set by the Root.

This parameter is conveyed to ensure that each Bridge in a Bridged Local Area Network has a consistent value against which to test the age of stored configuration information.

4.5.1.7 Hello Time. The time interval between the generation of Configuration BPDUs by the Root.

This parameter is not directly used by the Spanning Tree Algorithm but is conveyed in Configuration BPDUs to facilitate the monitoring of protocol performance by management functions.

4.5.1.8 Forward Delay. A timeout value to be used by all Bridges in the Bridged Local Area Network. The value of Forward Delay is set by the Root.

This parameter is conveyed to ensure that each Bridge in a Bridged Local Area Network uses a consistent value for the Forward Delay Timer when transferring the State of a Port to the Forwarding State. This parameter is also used as the timeout value for ageing Filtering Database dynamic entries following changes in active topology.

4.5.1.9 Topology Change Acknowledgment. A flag set by a Bridge which is the Designated Bridge for a LAN and which is transmitting a Configuration BPDU in response to a received Topology Change Notification BPDU.

This parameter is conveyed to allow a reliable acknowledged protocol to operate for the purpose of notifying the Root of changes in active topology.

4.5.1.10 Topology Change. A flag set by the Root in all Configuration BPDUs transmitted for a period of time following the notification or detection of a topology change.

This parameter is conveyed to notify Bridges throughout the Bridged Local Area Network that there has been a change in active topology in part of the Bridged Local Area Network and that the Filtering Database should age out entries more quickly in order to limit the effects of temporary isolation of end systems attached to the Bridged Local Area Network brought about by the use of incorrect information in the Filtering Database.

The value of the ageing time applied to dynamic entries in the Filtering Database becomes equal to that of the value of the Forward Delay time parameter held for the Bridge; i.e., after Forward Delay time has elapsed while the Topology Change flag is set in all Configuration Messages received from the Root, then the only dynamic entries remaining in the Filtering Database are those that have been created or updated during that period.

4.5.2 Topology Change Notification BPDU Parameters. No parameters are conveyed in a Topology Change Notification BPDU.

4.5.3 Bridge Parameters

4.5.3.1 Designated Root. The unique Bridge Identifier of the Bridge assumed to be the Root.

This parameter is used as the value of the Root Identifier parameter in all Configuration BPDUs transmitted by the Bridge.

4.5.3.2 Root Path Cost. The Cost of the path to the Root from this Bridge. It is equal to the sum of the values of the Designated Cost and Path Cost parameters held for the Root Port. When the Bridge is the Root this parameter has the value zero.

This parameter is used
(1) To test the value of the Root Path Cost parameter conveyed in received Configuration BPDUs.
(2) As the value of the Root Path Cost parameter offered in all Configuration BPDUs transmitted by the Bridge.

4.5.3.3 Root Port. The Port Identifier of the Port that offers the lowest cost path to the Root, i.e., that Port for which the sum of the values of the Designated Cost and Path Cost parameters held for the Port is the lowest.

If two or more Ports offer equal least cost paths to the Root, the Root Port is selected to be that with the highest priority Bridge Identifier held as the Designated Bridge Parameter for that Port.

If two or more Ports offer equal least cost paths to the Root and hold the same Designated Bridge parameter values, then the Root Port is selected to be that with the highest priority Designated Port held for that Port.

Finally, if two or more ports offer equal least cost paths to the Root and hold the same Designated Bridge and Designated Port parameter values, then the Root Port is selected to be that with the highest priority Port Identifier. The Port Identifiers for different Ports on the same Bridge are guaranteed to be different and thus enforce a tie-breaker.

This parameter is used to identify the Port through which the path to the Root is established. It is not significant when the Bridge is the Root, and is set to zero.

4.5.3.4 Max Age. The maximum age of received protocol information before it is discarded.

4.5.3.5 Hello Time. The time interval between the transmission of Configuration BPDUs by a Bridge that is attempting to become the Root or is the Root.

4.5.3.6 Forward Delay. The time spent in the Listening State while moving from the Blocking State to the Learning State.

The time spent in the Learning State while moving from the Listening State to the Forwarding State.

The value used for the ageing time of dynamic entries in the Filtering Database while the Topology Change flag is set in protocol messages received from the Root.

4.5.3.7 Bridge Identifier. The unique Bridge Identifier of the Bridge.

This parameter is used as the value of

(1) The Bridge Identifier parameter in all Configuration BPDUs transmitted by the Bridge.

(2) The Bridge's Designated Root when the Bridge is the Root, or when the Bridge attempts to become the Root, following expiry of all information concerning the current Root, or following management action.

This parameter comprises two parts, one of which is derived from the unique Bridge Address (3.12.5) and assures the uniqueness of the Bridge Identifier in the Bridged Local Area Network, the other of which allows the adjustment of the priority of the Bridge Identifier and is taken as the more significant part in priority comparisons. The priority part of this parameter may be updated by management action.

4.5.3.8 Bridge Max Age. The value of the Max Age parameter when the Bridge is the Root or is attempting to become the Root.

This parameter may be updated by management action.

4.5.3.9 Bridge Hello Time. The value of the Hello Time parameter when the Bridge is the Root or is attempting to become the Root.

The time interval between transmissions of Topology Change Notification BPDUs towards the Root when the Bridge is attempting to notify the Designated Bridge on the LAN to which its Root Port is attached of a topology change.

This parameter may be updated by management action.

4.5.3.10 Bridge Forward Delay. The value of the Forward Delay parameter when the Bridge is the Root or is attempting to become the Root.

This parameter may be updated by management action.

4.5.3.11 Topology Change Detected. A Boolean parameter set True to record a topology change that has been detected by or notified to the Bridge.

This parameter is used

(1) To stimulate regular transmissions, at intervals determined by the Bridge Hello Time, of a Topology Change Notification BPDU towards the Root where the Bridge itself is not the Root.

(2) If True, to set the value of the Topology Change parameter for the Bridge True if the Bridge is, or becomes, the Root.

4.5.3.12 Topology Change. A Boolean parameter set to record the value of the Topology Change flag in Configuration BPDUs to be transmitted by the Bridge on LANs for which the Bridge is the Designated Bridge.

If the value of this parameter is True, the timeout value of the Filtering Database ageing timer is equal to the value of the Forward Delay parameter. Dynamic entries whose age is greater than this value are removed from the Filtering Database.

If the value of this parameter is False, the timeout value of the Filtering Database ageing timer is equal to the value of the Ageing Time. Ageing Time may be set by management (Section 6).

4.5.3.13 Topology Change Time. The time period for which Bridge Protocol Data Units are transmitted with the Topology Change flag set by the Bridge when it is the Root following the detection of a topology change.

This value of this parameter is equal to the sum of the Bridge's Bridge Max Age and Bridge Forward Delay parameters. Either of these parameters may be updated by management action.

4.5.3.14 Hold Time. This parameter specifies the minimum time period elapsing between the transmission of Configuration BPDUs through a given Bridge Port. No more than two Configuration BPDUs shall be transmitted in any Hold Time time period.

This parameter is a fixed parameter of the Bridge. Its value is specified in Table 4-3.

4.5.4 Bridge Timers

4.5.4.1 Hello Timer. This timer serves to ensure periodic transmission of Configuration BPDUs by the Bridge when it is, or is attempting to become, the Root.

The timeout value of the timer is determined by the Bridge's Bridge Hello Time parameter.

4.5.4.2 Topology Change Notification Timer. This timer serves to ensure that the Designated Bridge on the LAN to which the Bridge's Root Port is attached is notified of any detected topology change.

The timeout value of the timer is determined by the Bridge's Bridge Hello Time parameter.

4.5.4.3 Topology Change Timer. This timer serves to determine the time period for which Configuration BPDUs are transmitted with the Topology Change flag set by the Bridge when it is the Root following the detection of a topology change.

The timeout value of the timer is determined by the Bridge's Topology Change Time parameter.

4.5.5 Port Parameters

4.5.5.1 Port Identifier. The Port Identifier of the associated Port.

This parameter is used as the value of the Port Identifier parameter of all Configuration BPDUs transmitted on the associated Port.

This parameter comprises two parts. One part bears a fixed relationship to the physical Ports supported by the real world equipment. Ports are identified by small integers from one upwards. This part of the parameter assures the uniqueness of the Port Identifier among the Ports of a single Bridge. The other part of the parameter allows the adjustment of the priority of the Port and is taken as the more significant part in priority comparisons. The priority part of this parameter may be updated by management action.

4.5.5.2 State. The current State of the Port (i.e., Disabled, Listening, Learning, Forwarding, or Blocking).

This parameter is used to control the acceptance of frames from the MAC Entity associated with the Port by the Forwarding and Learning Processes, the forwarding of frames by the Forwarding Process to that MAC Entity, and the transmission and reception of BPDUs (4.4).

This parameter is updated by the action of the protocol.

This parameter may also be updated by management action.

4.5.5.3 Path Cost. The contribution of the path through this Port, when the Port is the Root Port, to the total cost of the path to the Root for this Bridge.

This parameter is used, added to the value of the Designated Cost parameter for the Root Port, as the value of the Root Path Cost parameter offered in all Configuration BPDUs transmitted by the Bridge, when it is not the Root.

This parameter may be updated by management action.

4.5.5.4 Designated Root. The unique Bridge Identifier of the Bridge recorded as the Root in the Root Identifier parameter of Configuration BPDUs transmitted by the Designated Bridge for the LAN to which the Port is attached.

This parameter is used to test the value of the Root Identifier parameter conveyed in received Configuration BPDUs.

4.5.5.5 Designated Cost. The cost of the path to the Root offered by the Designated Port on the LAN to which this Port is attached.

This parameter is used to test the value of the Root Path Cost parameter conveyed in received Configuration BPDUs.

4.5.5.6 Designated Bridge. The unique Bridge Identifier of the Bridge believed to be the Designated Bridge for the LAN associated with the Port.

This parameter is used

(1) Together with the Designated Port and Port Identifier parameters for the Port to ascertain whether this Port should be the Designated Port for the LAN to which it is attached.

(2) To test the value of the Bridge Identifier parameter conveyed in received Configuration BPDUs.

4.5.5.7 Designated Port. The Port Identifier of the Bridge Port believed to be the Designated Port for the LAN associated with the Port.

This parameter is used

(1) Together with the Designated Bridge and Port Identifier parameters for the Port to ascertain whether this Port should be the Designated Port for the LAN to which it is attached.

(2) By management to determine the topology of the Bridged Local Area Network.

4.5.5.8 Topology Change Acknowledge. The value of the Topology Change Acknowledgment flag in the next Configuration BPDU to be transmitted on the associated Port.

This parameter is used to record the need to set the Topology Change Acknowledgment flag in reply to a received Topology Change Notification BPDU.

4.5.5.9 Configuration Pending. A Boolean parameter set to record that a Configuration BPDU should be transmitted on expiry of the Hold Timer for the associated Port.

This parameter is used, in conjunction with the Hold Timer for the Port, to ensure that Configuration BPDUs are not transmitted too frequently, but that up-to-date information is transmitted.

4.5.6 Port Timers

4.5.6.1 Message Age Timer. This timer serves to measure the age of the received protocol information recorded for a Port, and to ensure that this information is discarded when its age exceeds the value of the Max Age parameter recorded by the Bridge.

The timeout value of the timer is that of the Bridge's Max Age parameter.

4.5.6.2 Forward Delay Timer. This timer serves to monitor the time spent by a Port in the Listening and Learning States.

The timeout value of the timer is that of the Bridge's Forward Delay parameter.

4.5.6.3 Hold Timer. This timer serves to ensure that Configuration BPDUs are not transmitted too frequently through any Bridge Port.

The timeout value of the timer is that of the Hold Time for the Bridge.

4.6 Elements of Procedure

4.6.1 Transmit Configuration BPDU

4.6.1.1 Purpose. To convey knowledge of the Designated Root, Root Path Cost, Designated Bridge, Designated Port, and the values of protocol timers to other Bridge Ports attached to the same LAN as the Port on which the Configuration BPDU is transmitted.

4.6.1.2 Use

4.6.1.2.1 As part of the Configuration BPDU Generation procedure (4.6.4).

4.6.1.2.2 As part of the Reply to Configuration BPDU procedure (4.6.5).

4.6.1.2.3 Following expiry of the Hold Timer for the Port (4.7.8) when the Configuration Pending flag parameter for the Port is set, as a consequence of a previous invocation of the procedure.

4.6.1.2.4 As part of the Acknowledge Topology Change procedure (4.6.16).

4.6.1.3 Procedure

4.6.1.3.1 If the Hold Timer for the Port is active then the Configuration Pending flag parameter for the Port shall be set.

4.6.1.3.2 Otherwise, if the Hold Timer is not active, a Configuration BPDU shall be transmitted through the selected Port within a time maximum BPDU transmission delay (as specified in 4.10.2) after any invocation of this procedure.

The Configuration BPDU shall have parameters set as follows:

(1) The Configuration BPDU Root Identifier parameter shall be set to the value of the Designated Root parameter held by the Bridge.

(2) The Configuration BPDU Root Path Cost parameter shall be set to the value of the Root Path Cost parameter held by the Bridge.

(3) The Configuration BPDU Bridge Identifier parameter shall be set to the value of the Bridge Identifier parameter held by the Bridge.

(4) The Configuration BPDU Port Identifier parameter shall be set to the value of the Port Identifier parameter held for the Bridge Port through which the Configuration BPDU is transmitted.

(5) If the Bridge has been selected as the Root, i.e., if the values of the Designated Root and Bridge Identifier parameters held by the Bridge are the same, the Message Age parameter of the Configuration BPDU shall be set to zero.

(6) Otherwise, the value of the Message Age parameter shall be set such that the transmitted Configuration BPDU does not convey an underestimate of the age of the Protocol Message received on the Root Port; i.e., the value transmitted shall be no less than that recorded by the Message Age Timer for that Port, shall be greater than the value received, and will incorporate any transmission delay. The value of the parameter shall not exceed its true value by more than the maximum Message Age increment overestimate as specified in 4.10.2.

(7) The Max Age, Hello Time, and Forward Delay parameters of the Configuration BPDU shall be set to the values of the Max Age, Hello Time, and Forward Delay parameters held for the Bridge.

(8) The Configuration BPDU Topology Change Acknowledgment flag parameter shall be set to the value of the Topology Change Acknowledge flag parameter for the Port. The Topology Change Acknowledge parameter is reset.

(9) The Configuration BPDU Topology Change flag parameter shall be set to the value of the Topology Change flag parameter for the Bridge.

(10) The Configuration Pending flag parameter for the Port is reset.

(11) The Hold Timer for the Port is started.

4.6.2 Record Configuration Information

4.6.2.1 Purpose. To record, for a Port, protocol parameters conveyed by a Configuration BPDU received on that Port.

4.6.2.2 Use. Following the receipt of a Configuration BPDU conveying protocol information that supersedes that already held, i.e., if

4.6.2.2.1 The Root Identifier denotes a Bridge of higher priority than that recorded as the Designated Root, or

4.6.2.2.2 The Root Identifier is the same as the Designated Root, and the Root Path Cost is lower than that recorded as the Designated Cost for the Port, or

4.6.2.2.3 The Root Identifier and Root Path Cost are as recorded for the Port, and the Bridge Identifier denotes a Bridge of higher priority than that recorded as the Designated Bridge for the Port, or

4.6.2.2.4 The Root Identifier and Root Path Cost are as recorded for the Port, and the Bridge Identifier is the same as that recorded as the Designated Bridge for the Port, and either

(1) The Bridge receiving the BPDU is not the Designated Bridge for the Port, or
(2) The Port Identifier denotes a Port of priority not less than that recorded as the Designated Port.

4.6.2.3 Procedure

4.6.2.3.1 The Designated Root, Designated Cost, Designated Bridge, and Designated Port parameters held for the Port are set to the values of the Root Identifier, Root Path Cost, Bridge Identifier, and Port Identifier parameters conveyed in the received Configuration BPDU.

4.6.2.3.2 The Message Age Timer for the Port is started, to run from the value of the Message Age parameter conveyed in the received Configuration BPDU.

4.6.3 Record Configuration Timeout Values

4.6.3.1 Purpose. To update the Max Age, Hello Time, Forward Delay, and Topology Change flag parameters to the latest values received from the Root.

4.6.3.2 Use. Following receipt of a Configuration BPDU on the Root Port which invokes the Record Configuration Information procedure (4.6.2.2).

4.6.3.3 Procedure. The Max Age, Hello Time, Forward Delay, and Topology Change parameters held by the Bridge are set to the values conveyed in the received Configuration BPDU.

4.6.4 Configuration BPDU Generation

4.6.4.1 Purpose. To convey to Bridges attached to each LAN for which the Bridge is Designated Bridge knowledge of the Designated Root, Root Path Cost, Designated Bridge, Designated Port, and the values of protocol timers.

4.6.4.2 Use

4.6.4.2.1 Following receipt of a Configuration BPDU on the Root Port which invokes the Record Configuration Information procedure (4.6.2.2).

4.6.4.2.2 Following expiry of the Hello Timer.

4.6.4.2.3 Following selection of the Bridge as the Designated Root by the Configuration Update procedure on expiry of a Message Age Timer for a Bridge Port.

4.6.4.2.4 Following selection of the Bridge as the Designated Root by management action.

4.6.4.3 Procedure. For each Port that is the Designated Port for the LAN to which it is attached (i.e., the value of the Designated Bridge and Designated Port parameters held for the Port are the same as that of the Bridge Identifier and the Port Identifier for that Port, respectively, which is not in the Disabled State), the Transmit Configuration BPDU procedure (4.6.1) is used.

4.6.5 Reply to Configuration BPDU

4.6.5.1 Purpose. To establish the Designated Bridge and Designated Port for a LAN in the case where another Bridge Port has transmitted a Configuration BPDU on that LAN. This arises if Configuration Messages from the current Root have not been received by the transmitting Bridge, either due to that Root having been newly established or to BPDU loss and subsequent expiry of a Message Age Timer.

4.6.5.2 Use. Following receipt of a Configuration BPDU on a Port which is the Designated Port for the LAN to which it is attached, which does not update the information held for that Port, i.e., does not satisfy the conditions (4.6.2.2) for the use of the Record Configuration Information procedure.

4.6.5.3 Procedure. The Transmit Configuration BPDU procedure (4.6.1) is used for the Port on which the Configuration BPDU was received.

4.6.6 Transmit Topology Change Notification BPDU

4.6.6.1 Purpose. To notify the Bridge on the path towards the Root that an extension of the topology has been detected by the transmitting Bridge. Eventually this will result in the Root being notified of the topology change.

4.6.6.2 Use

4.6.6.2.1 Following the detection or receipt of notification of a topology change by a Bridge that is not the Root.

4.6.6.2.2 Following expiry of the Topology Change Notification Timer.

4.6.6.3 Procedure. A Topology Change Notification BPDU shall be transmitted through the Root Port within a time of maximum BPDU transmission delay (4.10.2).

4.6.7 Configuration Update

4.6.7.1 Purpose. To update the configuration information held by the Bridge and the Bridge Ports.

4.6.7.2 Use

4.6.7.2.1 Following receipt of a Configuration BPDU which invokes the Record Configuration Information procedure (4.6.2.2).

4.6.7.2.2 Following a Port becoming the Designated Port for the LAN to which it is attached on expiry of the Message Age Timer for that Port.

4.6.7.2.3 Following a change in Port State through management action.

4.6.7.3 Procedure

4.6.7.3.1 The procedure for Root Selection (4.6.8) shall be used to select the Designated Root and the Root Port, and to calculate the Root Path Cost for this Bridge.

4.6.7.3.2 The procedure for Designated Port Selection (4.6.9) shall be used to determine for each Port whether the Port should become the Designated Port for the LAN to which it is attached.

4.6.8 Root Selection

4.6.8.1 Purpose. To select the Designated Root and the Root Port, and to calculate the Root Path Cost for this Bridge.

4.6.8.2 Use. This procedure is used by the Configuration Update procedure (4.6.7).

4.6.8.3 Procedure

4.6.8.3.1 The Root Port is set to identify the Port which; among those that are not the Designated Port for the LAN to which they are attached, are not Disabled, and have a Designated Root parameter of higher priority than the Bridge's Bridge Identifier;

(1) Has the highest priority Root associated with it, i.e., recorded as the Designated Root for the Port.

(2) Of two or more Ports with the highest priority Designated Root parameter, has the lowest Root Path Cost associated with it, i.e., the lowest sum of the Designated Cost and Path Cost parameters for any Port, or

(3) Of two or more Ports with the highest priority Designated Root parameter and lowest value of associated Root Path Cost, has the highest priority Bridge Identifier recorded as the Designated Bridge for the LAN to which the Port is attached, or

(4) Of two or more Ports with the highest priority Designated Root parameter, lowest value of associated Root Path Cost, and highest priority Designated Bridge, has the highest priority Port Identifier recorded as the Designated Port for the LAN to which the Port is attached, or

(5) Of two or more Ports with the highest priority Designated Root parameter, lowest value of associated Root Path Cost, and highest priority Designated Bridge and Designated Port, has the highest priority Port Identifier.

4.6.8.3.2 If there is no such Port, the value of the Root Port parameter is set to Zero, and

(1) The Designated Root parameter held by the Bridge is set to the Bridge Identifier parameter held for the Bridge, and

(2) The value of the Root Path Cost parameter held by the Bridge is set to zero.

4.6.8.3.3 Otherwise, i.e., if one of the Bridge Ports has been identified as the Root Port, then

(1) The Designated Root parameter held by the Bridge is set to the Designated Root parameter held for the Root Port, and

(2) The value of the Root Path Cost parameter held by the Bridge is set to the value of the Root Path Cost parameter associated with the Root Port, i.e., the sum of the values of the Path Cost and the Designated Cost parameters recorded for the Root Port.

4.6.9 Designated Port Selection

4.6.9.1 Purpose. To determine, for each Port, whether the Port should be the Designated Port for the LAN to which it is attached.

4.6.9.2 Use. As part of the Configuration Update procedure (4.6.7).

4.6.9.3 Procedure. The procedure to Become Designated Port (4.6.10) shall be invoked for each Port that

4.6.9.3.1 Has already been selected as the Designated Port for the LAN to which it is attached, i.e., the value of the Designated Bridge and Designated Port parameters held for the Port are the same as that of the Bridge Identifier and the Port Identifier for that Port respectively, or for which

4.6.9.3.2 The Designated Root parameter recorded for the Bridge differs from that recorded for the Port (note that this procedure follows root selection), or

4.6.9.3.3 The Bridge offers a Path of lower Cost to the Root for the LAN to which the Port is attached, i.e., the Root Path Cost recorded by the Bridge is less than the Designated Cost recorded for the Port, or

4.6.9.3.4 The Bridge offers a Path of equal Cost to the Root, and the Bridge's Bridge Identifier denotes a Bridge of higher priority than that recorded as the Designated Bridge for that Port, or

4.6.9.3.5 The Bridge offers a Path of equal Cost to the Root, and the Bridge is the Designated Bridge for the LAN to which the Port is attached, and the Port Identifier of the Port is of higher priority than that recorded as the Designated Port.

4.6.10 Become Designated Port

4.6.10.1 Purpose. Given that a Port is to be the Designated Port on the LAN to which it is attached, to assign appropriate values to those Port parameters that determine the active topology of the Bridged Local Area Network.

4.6.10.2 Use

4.6.10.2.1 Following expiry of the Message Age Timer for the Port.

4.6.10.2.2 Following selection of the Port as the Designated Port for the LAN to which it is attached by the Designated Port Selection procedure (4.6.9) as part of the Configuration Update procedure (4.6.7).

4.6.10.2.3 Following a change of Port State through management action (4.8.1, 4.8.2, 4.8.3, 4.8.5).

4.6.10.3 Procedure

4.6.10.3.1 The Designated Root parameter held for the Port is set to the value of the Designated Root parameter held by the Bridge.

4.6.10.3.2 The Designated Cost parameter held for the Port is set to the value of the Root Path Cost held by the Bridge.

4.6.10.3.3 The Designated Bridge parameter held for the Port is set to the Bridge Identifier of the Bridge.

4.6.10.3.4 The Designated Port parameter held for the Port is set to the Port Identifier of the Port.

4.6.11 Port State Selection

4.6.11.1 Purpose. To select the State of the Bridge's Ports based upon updated configuration information which indicates, for each Port, its part in the active topology of the Bridged Local Area Network, i.e., whether it should

(1) Be the Root Port for the Bridge.
(2) Be a Designated Port.
(3) Be a backup Port in a redundantly connected Bridged Local Area Network.

4.6.11.2 Use. Following use of the Configuration Update procedure after

4.6.11.2.1 Receipt of a Configuration BPDU conveying information that supersedes that recorded for a Port.

4.6.11.2.2 The expiry of the Message Age timer for a Port, which causes that Port to become the Designated Port for the LAN to which it is attached.

4.6.11.2.3 A change in the State of a Port arising through management action.

4.6.11.3 Procedure. For each of the Bridge's Ports:

4.6.11.3.1 If the Port is the Root Port for the Bridge, then

(1) The Configuration Pending flag parameter and Topology Change Acknowledge flag parameter for the Port are reset.
(2) The Make Forwarding procedure (4.6.12) is used for the Port.

4.6.11.3.2 Otherwise, if the Port is the Designated Port for the LAN to which it is attached, i.e., the Designated Bridge parameter for the Port is the same as the Bridge Identifier parameter held by the Bridge, and the Designated Port and Port Identifier parameters held for the Port are the same and the Port is not in the Disabled State, then

(1) The Message Age Timer for the Port is stopped, if running.
(2) The Make Forwarding procedure (4.6.12) is used for the Port.

4.6.11.3.3 Otherwise, if the Port is to be a backup Port, i.e., is neither the Root Port or a Designated Port, then

(1) The Configuration Pending flag parameter and Topology Change Acknowledge flag parameter for the Port are reset.

(2) The procedure to Make Blocking (4.6.13) is used.

4.6.12 Make Forwarding

4.6.12.1 Purpose. To permit a Port to participate in frame relay, following a suitable interval which ensures that temporary loops in the Bridged Local Area Network do not cause duplication of frames.

4.6.12.2 Use. As part of the Port State Selection procedure (4.6.11).

4.6.12.3 Procedure. If the Port State is Blocking, then

4.6.12.3.1 The Port State is set to Listening, and

4.6.12.3.2 The Forward Delay Timer for the Port is started.

4.6.13 Make Blocking

4.6.13.1 Purpose. To terminate the participation of a Port in frame relay.

4.6.13.2 Use. As part of the Port State Selection procedure (4.6.11).

4.6.13.3 Procedure. If the Port is not in the Disabled or the Blocking State, then

4.6.13.3.1 If the Port is in the Forwarding or Learning State, the Topology Change Detection procedure (4.6.14) is invoked.

4.6.13.3.2 The Port State for the Port is set to Blocking.

4.6.13.3.3 The Forward Delay Timer for the Port is stopped.

4.6.14 Topology Change Detection

4.6.14.1 Purpose. To record a topology change that has been detected by or notified to the Bridge. To initiate action to communicate the fact that a topology change has been detected to the Root.

4.6.14.2 Use

4.6.14.2.1 On receipt of a Topology Change Notification BPDU on a Port that is the Designated Port for the LAN to which it is attached.

4.6.14.2.2 When a Bridge Port is put into the Forwarding State following the expiry of the Forward Delay Timer for the Port, provided that the Bridge is the Designated Bridge for at least one of the LANs to which its Ports are attached.

4.6.14.2.3 When a Bridge Port in either the Forwarding or the Learning State is put into the Blocking State.

4.6.14.2.4 When the Bridge becomes the Root.

4.6.14.3 Procedure

4.6.14.3.1 If the Bridge has been selected as the Root, i.e., the Designated Root and Bridge Identifier parameters held for the Bridge are the same, then

(1) The Topology Change flag parameter held for the Bridge is set.

(2) The Topology Change Timer for the Bridge is started.

4.6.14.3.2 If the Bridge has not been selected as the Root and the Topology Change Detected flag parameter held for the Bridge is not already set, then

(1) The Transmit Topology Change Notification BPDU procedure (4.6.6) is invoked.

(2) The Topology Change Notification Timer is started.

4.6.14.3.3 The Topology Change Detected flag parameter for the Bridge is set.

4.6.15 Topology Change Acknowledged

4.6.15.1 Purpose. To terminate the transmission of Topology Change Notification BPDUs.

4.6.15.2 Use. Following receipt of a Configuration BPDU with the Topology Change Acknowledgment flag parameter set from the Designated Bridge for the LAN to which the Root Port is attached.

4.6.15.3 Procedure

4.6.15.3.1 The Topology Change Detected flag parameter held for the Bridge is reset.

4.6.15.3.2 The Topology Change Notification Timer is stopped.

4.6.16 Acknowledge Topology Change

4.6.16.1 Purpose. To acknowledge the notification of a detected topology change by another Bridge.

4.6.16.2 Use. Following receipt of a Topology Change Notification BPDU on a Port which is the Designated Port for the LAN to which it is attached.

4.6.16.3 Procedure

4.6.16.3.1 The Topology Change Acknowledge flag parameter for the Port is set.

4.6.16.3.2 The Transmit Configuration BPDU procedure (4.6.1) is used for the Port.

4.7 Operation of the Protocol. A Bridge Protocol Entity shall

(1) Communicate with its Peer Entities in other Bridges by the transmission of Bridge Protocol Data Units;

(2) Update stored protocol variables and timers;

(3) Change the State of the Bridge Ports;

following

(a) The reception of Bridge Protocol Data Units;

(b) The expiry of Bridge and Port Timers;

as required by the specification below (4.7.1, 4.7.2, 4.7.3, 4.7.4, 4.7.5, 4.7.6, 4.7.7, 4.7.8). In any case of ambiguity, reference shall be made to the Procedural Model (4.9), which constitutes the definitive description of the operation of the protocol.

This specification uses the Elements of Procedure of the Protocol described in 4.6, which, taken together with this subsection and the Protocol Parameters and Timers described in 4.5, provide an abstract description of the Spanning Tree Algorithm and Protocol. Conformance to this specification is achieved through maintenance of the Protocol Parameters and Timers and the transmission of BPDUs as described. Implementations are not otherwise constrained, in particular there is no conformance to individual elements of procedure.

4.7.1 Received Configuration BPDU

4.7.1.1 If the Configuration BPDU received conveys protocol information that supersedes that already held for a Port as specified in 4.6.2.2, then the following sequence of Procedures is used:

4.7.1.1.1 The Record Configuration Information procedure (4.6.2).

4.7.1.1.2 The Configuration Update procedure (4.6.7).

4.7.1.1.3 The Port State Selection procedure (4.6.11).

4.7.1.1.4 If the Bridge was selected as the Root prior to Configuration Update, but is no longer, then the Hello Timer (4.5.4.1) is stopped.

4.7.1.1.5 If the Bridge was selected as the Root prior to Configuration Update, but is no longer, and the Topology Change Detected flag parameter is set, then the Topology Change Timer is stopped, the Transmit Topology Change Notification BPDU procedure (4.6.6) is used, and the Topology Change Notification Timer is started.

4.7.1.1.6 If the Configuration BPDU was received on the Root Port (i.e., the Port selected as the Root Port by the Configuration Update procedure), the Record Configuration Timeout Values (4.6.3) and the Configuration BPDU Generation (4.6.4) procedures.

4.7.1.1.7 If the Configuration BPDU was received on the Root Port and the Topology Change Acknowledgment flag parameter was set, the Topology Change Acknowledged procedure (4.6.15).

4.7.1.2 If the Configuration BPDU received does not convey information superseding that already held for the Port and that Port is the Designated Port for the LAN to which it is attached, i.e., the value of the Designated Bridge and Designated Port parameters held for the Port are the same as that of the Bridge Identifier for the Bridge and the Port Identifier for that Port respectively, then

4.7.1.2.1 The Reply to Configuration BPDU procedure (4.6.5) is used.

4.7.2 Received Topology Change Notification BPDU. If the Port on which the Topology Change Notification BPDU was received is the Designated Port for the LAN to which it is attached, then

4.7.2.1 The Topology Change Detection procedure (4.6.14) is used.

4.7.2.2 The Acknowledge Topology Change procedure (4.6.16) is used.

4.7.3 Hello Timer Expiry. The Configuration BPDU Generation procedure (4.6.4) is used and the Hello Timer (4.5.4.1) is started.

4.7.4 Message Age Timer Expiry

4.7.4.1 The procedure to Become Designated Port (4.6.10) is used for the Port for which Message Age Timer has expired.

4.7.4.2 The Configuration Update procedure (4.6.7) is used.

4.7.4.3 The Port State Selection procedure (4.6.11) is used.

4.7.4.4 If the Bridge is selected as the Root following Configuration Update, then

4.7.4.4.1 The Max Age, Hello Time, and Forward Delay parameters held by the Bridge are set to the values of the Bridge Max Age, Bridge Hello Time, and Bridge Forward Delay parameters.

4.7.4.4.2 The Topology Change Detection procedure (4.6.14) is used.

4.7.4.4.3 The Topology Change Notification Timer (4.5.4.2) is stopped.

4.7.4.4.4 The Configuration BPDU Generation procedure (4.6.4) is used and the Hello Timer is started.

4.7.5 Forward Delay Timer Expiry

4.7.5.1 If the State of the Port for which the Forward Delay Timer (4.5.6.2) has expired was Listening, then

4.7.5.1.1 The Port State is set to Learning, and

4.7.5.1.2 The Forward Delay Timer is restarted.

4.7.5.2 Otherwise, if the State of the Port for which the Forward Delay Timer (4.5.6.2) has expired was Learning, then

4.7.5.2.1 The Port State is set to Forwarding, and

4.7.5.2.2 If the Bridge is the Designated Bridge for at least one of the LANs to which its Ports are attached, the Topology Change Detection procedure (4.6.14) is invoked.

4.7.6 Topology Change Notification Timer Expiry

4.7.6.1 The Transmit Topology Change Notification BPDU procedure (4.6.6) is used.

4.7.6.2 The Topology Change Notification Timer (4.5.4.2) is restarted.

4.7.7 Topology Change Timer Expiry

4.7.7.1 The Topology Change Detected flag parameter held by the Bridge is reset.

4.7.7.2 The Topology Change flag parameter held by the Bridge is reset.

4.7.8 Hold Timer Expiry. If the Configuration Pending flag parameter for the Port for which the Hold Timer (4.5.6.3) has expired is set, the Transmit Configuration BPDU procedure (4.6.1) is invoked for that Port.

4.8 Management of the Bridge Protocol Entity. Management control of the Bridge Protocol Entity, which operates the Spanning Tree Algorithm and Protocol, may be exerted in order to

(1) Meet any requirements for local information and configuration services.

(2) Support management operations.

This section specifies the interaction of the following management operations with the parameters and procedures of the Spanning Tree Algorithm and Protocol:

(a) Initialization

(b) Enabling an individual Port

(c) Disabling an individual Port

(d) Changing the priority part of a Bridge Identifier

(e) Changing the priority part of a Port Identifier

(f) Change the Path Cost associated with an individual Port

These operations shall modify the Protocol Parameters and Timers and transmit BPDUs as described below (4.8.1, 4.8.2, 4.8.3, 4.8.4, 4.8.5, 4.8.6). Implementations are not otherwise constrained; in particular, there is no conformance to individual elements of procedure. In any case of ambiguity, reference shall be made to the Procedural Model (4.9), which constitutes the definitive description of these operations.

This section does not specify which operations are made available to a remote management station, nor how these are combined and conveyed. Operations and facilities that can be provided by remote management are detailed in Section 6. Similarly, this section does not specify the availability of local information and configuration procedures.

4.8.1 Initialization

4.8.1.1 The Designated Root parameter held for the Bridge is set equal to the value of the Bridge Identifier, and the value of the Root Path Cost parameter held for the Bridge is set to zero.

4.8.1.2 The Max Age, Hello Time, and Forward Delay parameters held by the Bridge are set to the values of the Bridge Max Age, Bridge Hello Time, and Bridge Forward Delay parameters.

4.8.1.3 The Topology Change Detected and Topology Change flag parameters for the Bridge are reset, and the Topology Change Notification Timer (4.5.4.2) and Topology Change Timer (4.5.4.3) are stopped, if running.

4.8.1.4 For each of the Bridge's Ports

4.8.1.4.1 The Become Designated Port procedure (4.6.10) is used to assign values to the Designated Root, Designated Cost, Designated Bridge, and Designated Port parameters for the Port.

4.8.1.4.2 The Port State is set to Blocking if the Port is to be enabled following initialization; alternatively, the Port State is set to Disabled.

4.8.1.4.3 The Topology Change Acknowledge flag parameter is reset.

4.8.1.4.4 The Configuration Pending flag parameter is reset.

4.8.1.4.5 The Message Age Timer (4.5.6.1) is stopped, if running.

4.8.1.4.6 The Forward Delay Timer (4.5.6.2) is stopped, if running.

4.8.1.4.7 The Hold Timer (4.5.6.3) is stopped, if running.

4.8.1.5 The Port State Selection procedure (4.6.11) is used to select the State of each of the Bridge's Ports.

4.8.1.6 The Configuration BPDU Generation procedure (4.6.4) is invoked and the Hello Timer (4.5.4.1) started.

4.8.2 Enable Port

4.8.2.1 The Become Designated Port procedure (4.6.10) is used to assign values to the Designated Root, Designated Cost, Designated Bridge, and Designated Port parameters for the Port.

4.8.2.2 The Port State is set to Blocking.

4.8.2.3 The Topology Change Acknowledge flag parameter is reset.

4.8.2.4 The Configuration Pending flag parameter is reset.

4.8.2.5 The Message Age Timer (4.5.6.1) is stopped, if running.

4.8.2.6 The Forward Delay Timer (4.5.6.2) is stopped, if running.

4.8.2.7 The Hold Timer (4.5.6.3) is stopped, if running.

4.8.2.8 The Port State Selection procedure (4.6.11) is used.

4.8.3 Disable Port

4.8.3.1 The Become Designated Port procedure (4.6.10) is used to assign values to the Designated Root, Designated Cost, Designated Bridge, and Designated Port parameters for the Port.

4.8.3.2 The Port State is set to Disabled.

4.8.3.3 The Topology Change Acknowledge flag parameter is reset.

4.8.3.4 The Configuration Pending flag parameter is reset.

4.8.3.5 The Message Age Timer (4.5.6.1) is stopped, if running.

4.8.3.6 The Forward Delay Timer (4.5.6.2) is stopped, if running.

4.8.3.7 The Configuration Update procedure (4.6.7) is used.

4.8.3.8 The Port State Selection procedure (4.6.11) is used.

4.8.3.9 If the Bridge has been selected as the Root following Configuration Update, then

4.8.3.9.1 The Max Age, Hello Time, and Forward Delay parameters held by the Bridge are set to the values of the Bridge Max Age, Bridge Hello Time, and Bridge Forward Delay parameters.

4.8.3.9.2 The Topology Change Detection procedure (4.6.14) is used.

4.8.3.9.3 The Topology Change Notification Timer (4.5.4.2) is stopped.

4.8.3.9.4 The Configuration BPDU Generation procedure (4.6.4) is used and the Hello Timer is started.

4.8.4 Set Bridge Priority

4.8.4.1 The new value of the Bridge Identifier is calculated.

4.8.4.2 The value of the Designated Bridge parameter held for each Port that has been selected as the Designated Port for the LAN to which it is attached; i.e., for which the value of the Designated Bridge and Designated Port parameters were the same as that of the Bridge Identifier and the Port Identifier for that Port, respectively; is set to the new value of the Bridge Identifier.

4.8.4.3 The Bridge Identifier parameter held by the Bridge is set to the new value.

4.8.4.4 The Configuration Update procedure (4.6.7) is used.

4.8.4.5 The Port State Selection procedure (4.6.11) is used.

4.8.4.6 If the Bridge has been selected as the Root following Configuration Update, then

4.8.4.6.1 The Max Age, Hello Time, and Forward Delay parameters held by the Bridge are set to the values of the Bridge Max Age, Bridge Hello Time, and Bridge Forward Delay parameters.

4.8.4.6.2 The Topology Change Detection procedure (4.6.14) is used.

4.8.4.6.3 The Topology Change Notification Timer (4.5.4.2) is stopped.

4.8.4.6.4 The Configuration BPDU Generation procedure (4.6.4) is used and the Hello Timer is started.

4.8.5 Set Port Priority

4.8.5.1 The new value of the Port Identifier is calculated.

4.8.5.2 If the Port has been selected as the Designated Port for the LAN to which it is attached; i.e., the value of the Designated Bridge and Designated Port parameters were the same as that of the Bridge Identifier and the Port Identifier, respectively; the Designated Port parameter held for the Port is set to the new value of the Port Identifier.

4.8.5.3 The Port Identifier parameter held for the Port is set to the new value.

4.8.5.4 If the value of the Designated Bridge parameter held for the Port is equal to that of the Bridge's Bridge Identifier, and the new value of the Port Identifier is of higher priority than that recorded as the Designated Port, then

4.8.5.4.1 The Become Designated Port procedure (4.6.10) is used to assign values to the Designated Root, Designated Cost, Designated Bridge, and Designated Port parameters for the Port.

4.8.5.4.2 The Port State Selection procedure (4.6.11) is used.

4.8.6 Set Path Cost

4.8.6.1 The Path Cost parameter for the Port is set to the new value.

4.8.6.2 The Configuration Update procedure (4.6.7) is used.

4.8.6.3 The Port State Selection procedure is used.

4.9 Procedural Model. This subsection constitutes the definitive description of the operation of the Spanning Tree Algorithm and Protocol. The natural language text in 4.6, 4.7, and 4.8 of this standard is intended to informally present the semantics of operation specified here. Should differences of interpretation exist between that text and this procedural model, the latter shall take precedence.

4.9.1 Overview. The parameters, timers, elements of procedure, and operation of the protocol are presented below as a compilable program in the computer language C (ANSI X3.159 [1]).

The objective of presenting this program is to precisely and unambiguously specify the operation of the algorithm and protocol. The description of the operation of the protocol in a computer language is in no way intended to constrain the implementation of the protocol; a real implementation may employ any appropriate technology.

Conformance of equipment to this standard is purely in respect of observable protocol. The program contained in this section contains modeling details that are of local concern to an implementation; there is no conformance in respect of these details.

The natural language text in 4.6, 4.7, 4.8 follows the computer language text contained in this section. In order to preserve the compactness of the program text, all comments are made by reference to the natural language description and are of the form 4.n.n.n. Where a program statement invokes an element of procedure, a further reference is made to the particular condition, of those listed for the procedure, that has caused the procedure to be invoked.

```
/******************************************************************************
 *
 *  SPANNING TREE ALGORITHM AND PROTOCOL
 *
 ******************************************************************************/


/******************************************************************************
 *  DEFINED CONSTANTS
 ******************************************************************************/

#define Zero        0
#define One         1

#define False       0
#define True        1

/** port states. **/

#define Disabled       0                              /* (4.4.5)      */
#define Listening      1                              /* (4.4.2)      */
#define Learning       2                              /* (4.4.3)      */
#define Forwarding     3                              /* (4.4.4)      */
#define Blocking       4                              /* (4.4.1)      */

/** BPDU type constants **/

#define Config_bpdu_type    0
#define Tcn_bpdu_type       128

/** pseudo-implementation constants. **/

#define No_of_ports 2
        /* arbitrary choice, to allow the code below to compile */

#define All_ports No_of_ports+1
        /* ports start at 1, arrays in C start at 0 */

#define Default_path_cost 10
        /* arbitrary */

#define Message_age_increment 1
        /* minimum increment possible to avoid underestimating age, allows
           for BPDU transmission time */

#define No_port 0
        /* reserved value for Bridge's root port parameter indicating no
           root port, used when Bridge is the root */
```

78

```
/*******************************************************************************
* TYPEDEFS, STRUCTURES, AND UNION DECLARATIONS
*******************************************************************************/

/** basic types. **/

typedef int Int;          /* to align with case stropping convention used
                             here. Types and defined constants have their
                             initial letters capitalised. */

typedef Int Boolean;      /* : (True, False) */

typedef Int State;        /* : (Disabled, Listening, Learning,
                                 Forwarding, Blocking) */


/** BPDU encoding types defined in Section 5. "Encoding of Bridge Protocol
Data Units" are:

Protocol_version    (5.2.2)

Bpdu_type           (5.2.3)

Flag                (5.2.4)

Identifier          (5.2.5)

Cost                (5.2.6)

Port_id             (5.2.7)

Time                (5.2.8)

**/

#include "types.c"      /* defines BPDU encoding types */
```

```
/** Configuration BPDU Parameters (4.5.1) **/

typedef struct
{
  Bpdu_type  type;

  Identifier root_id;                              /* (4.5.1.1)    */

  Cost       root_path_cost;                       /* (4.5.1.2)    */

  Identifier bridge_id;                            /* (4.5.1.3)    */

  Port_id    port_id;                              /* (4.5.1.4)    */

  Time       message_age;                          /* (4.5.1.5)    */

  Time       max_age;                              /* (4.5.1.6)    */

  Time       hello_time;                           /* (4.5.1.7)    */

  Time       forward_delay;                        /* (4.5.1.8)    */

  Flag       topology_change_acknowledgment;       /* (4.5.1.9)    */

  Flag       topology_change;                      /* (4.5.1.10)   */

} Config_bpdu;


/** Topology Change Notification BPDU Parameters (4.5.2) **/

typedef struct
{
  Bpdu_type  type;

} Tcn_bpdu;
```

```
/** Bridge Parameters (4.5.3) **/

typedef struct
{
    Identifier designated_root;                 /* (4.5.3.1)   */

    Cost       root_path_cost;                  /* (4.5.3.2)   */

    Int        root_port;                       /* (4.5.3.3)   */

    Time       max_age;                         /* (4.5.3.4)   */

    Time       hello_time;                      /* (4.5.3.5)   */

    Time       forward_delay;                   /* (4.5.3.6)   */

    Identifier bridge_id;                       /* (4.5.3.7)   */

    Time       bridge_max_age;                  /* (4.5.3.8)   */

    Time       bridge_hello_time;               /* (4.5.3.9)   */

    Time       bridge_forward_delay;            /* (4.5.3.10)  */

    Boolean    topology_change_detected;        /* (4.5.3.11)  */

    Boolean    topology_change;                 /* (4.5.3.12)  */

    Time       topology_change_time;            /* (4.5.3.13)  */

    Time       hold_time;                       /* (4.5.3.14)  */

} Bridge_data;
```

```
/** Port Parameters (4.5.5) **/

typedef struct
{
    Port_id     port_id;                             /* (4.5.5.1)    */

    State       state;                               /* (4.5.5.2)    */

    Int         path_cost;                           /* (4.5.5.3)    */

    Identifier designated_root;                      /* (4.5.5.4)    */

    Int         designated_cost;                     /* (4.5.5.5)    */

    Identifier designated_bridge;                    /* (4.5.5.6)    */

    Port_id     designated_port;                     /* (4.5.5.7)    */

    Boolean     topology_change_acknowledge;         /* (4.5.5.8)    */

    Boolean     config_pending;                      /* (4.5.5.9)    */

} Port_data ;
```

```
/** types to support timers for this pseudo-implementation. **/

typedef struct
{
    Boolean    active;         /* timer in use. */

    Time       value;          /* current value of timer, counting up. */

} Timer;



/*******************************************************************************
 * STATIC STORAGE ALLOCATION
 ******************************************************************************/


Bridge_data    bridge_info;                            /* (4.5.3)       */

Port_data      port_info[All_ports];                   /* (4.5.5)       */

Config_bpdu    config_bpdu[All_ports];

Tcn_bpdu       tcn_bpdu[All_ports];

Timer          hello_timer;                            /* (4.5.4.1)     */

Timer          tcn_timer;                              /* (4.5.4.2)     */

Timer          topology_change_timer;                  /* (4.5.4.3)     */

Timer          message_age_timer[All_ports];           /* (4.5.6.1)     */

Timer          forward_delay_timer[All_ports];         /* (4.5.6.2)     */

Timer          hold_timer[All_ports];                  /* (4.5.6.3)     */
```

```
/*******************************************************************************
*  CODE
*******************************************************************************/

/** Elements of Procedure (4.6) **/

transmit_config(port_no)                                /* (4.6.1)       */
Int     port_no;
{
   if (hold_timer[port_no].active)                      /* (4.6.1.3.1)   */
   {
      port_info[port_no].config_pending = True;         /* (4.6.1.3.1)   */
   }
   else                                                 /* (4.6.1.3.2)   */
   {
      config_bpdu[port_no].type = Config_bpdu_type;

      config_bpdu[port_no].root_id = bridge_info.designated_root;
                                                        /* (4.6.1.3.2(1)) */
      config_bpdu[port_no].root_path_cost = bridge_info.root_path_cost;
                                                        /* (4.6.1.3.2(2)) */
      config_bpdu[port_no].bridge_id = bridge_info.bridge_id;
                                                        /* (4.6.1.3.2(3)) */
      config_bpdu[port_no].port_id = port_info[port_no].port_id;
                                                        /* (4.6.1.3.2(4)) */
      if (root_bridge())
      {
         config_bpdu[port_no].message_age = Zero;       /* (4.6.1.3.2(5)) */
      }
      else
      {
         config_bpdu[port_no].message_age
           = message_age_timer[bridge_info.root_port].value
              + Message_age_increment;                  /* (4.6.1.3.2(6)) */
      }

      config_bpdu[port_no].max_age = bridge_info.max_age;  /* (4.6.1.3.2(7)) */
      config_bpdu[port_no].hello_time = bridge_info.hello_time;
      config_bpdu[port_no].forward_delay = bridge_info.forward_delay;

      config_bpdu[port_no].topology_change_acknowledgment
        = port_info[port_no].topology_change_acknowledge;
                                                        /* (4.6.1.3.2(8)) */
      port_info[port_no].topology_change_acknowledge = False;
                                                        /* (4.6.1.3.2(8)) */
      config_bpdu[port_no].topology_change
        = bridge_info.topology_change;                  /* (4.6.1.3.2(9)) */

      send_config_bpdu(port_no, &config_bpdu[port_no]);

      port_info[port_no].config_pending = False;        /* (4.6.1.3.2(10))*/

      start_hold_timer(port_no);                        /* (4.6.1.3.2(11))*/
   }

   }
```

```
/* where

send_config_bpdu(port_no,bpdu)
Int         port_no;
Config_bpdu *bpdu;

is a pseudo-implementation-specific routine which transmits
the bpdu on the specified port within the specified time.

*/

/* and */

Boolean root_bridge()
{
    return(bridge_info.designated_root == bridge_info.bridge_id);
}
```

```
Boolean supersedes_port_info(port_no, config)          /* (4.6.2.2)     */
Int port_no;
Config_bpdu *config;
{
   return (
   ( config->root_id
     < port_info[port_no].designated_root                /* (4.6.2.2.1)   */
   )
   ||
   ( ( config->root_id
       == port_info[port_no].designated_root
     )
     &&
     ( ( config->root_path_cost
         < port_info[port_no].designated_cost            /* (4.6.2.2.2)   */
       )
       ||
       ( ( config->root_path_cost
           == port_info[port_no].designated_cost
         )
         &&
         ( ( config->bridge_id
             < port_info[port_no].designated_bridge      /* (4.6.2.2.3)   */
           )
           ||
           ( ( config->bridge_id
               == port_info[port_no].designated_bridge
             )                                            /* (4.6.2.2.4)   */
             &&
             ( ( config->bridge_id != bridge_info.bridge_id
               )                                          /* (4.6.2.2.4(1)) */
               ||
               ( config->port_id
                 <= port_info[port_no].designated_port
               )                                          /* (4.6.2.2.4(2)) */
   ) ) ) ) ) )
         );
}


record_config_information(port_no, config)               /* (4.6.2)       */
Int port_no;
Config_bpdu *config;
{
   port_info[port_no].designated_root = config->root_id;    /* (4.6.2.3.1)   */
   port_info[port_no].designated_cost = config->root_path_cost;
   port_info[port_no].designated_bridge = config->bridge_id;
   port_info[port_no].designated_port = config->port_id;

   start_message_age_timer(port_no, config->message_age);   /* (4.6.2.3.2)   */
}
```

```
record_config_timeout_values(config)                          /* (4.6.3)      */
Config_bpdu *config;
{
    bridge_info.max_age = config->max_age;                     /* (4.6.3.3)    */
    bridge_info.hello_time = config->hello_time;
    bridge_info.forward_delay = config->forward_delay;
    bridge_info.topology_change = config->topology_change;
}



config_bpdu_generation()                                      /* (4.6.4)      */
{
    Int port_no;

    for (port_no = One; port_no <= No_of_ports; port_no++)    /* (4.6.4.3)    */
    {
        if (  designated_port(port_no)                        /* (4.6.4.3)    */
              &&
              (port_info[port_no].state != Disabled)
           )
        {
            transmit_config(port_no);                         /* (4.6.4.3)    */
        }                                                     /* (4.6.1.2)    */
    }
}


        /* where */

        Boolean designated_port(port_no)
        Int port_no;
        {
            return ( (  port_info[port_no].designated_bridge
                        == bridge_info.bridge_id
                     )
                     &&
                     (  port_info[port_no].designated_port
                        == port_info[port_no].port_id
                     )
                   );
        }
```

```
reply(port_no)                                          /* (4.6.5)         */
Int port_no;
{
   transmit_config(port_no);                            /* (4.6.5.3)       */
}


transmit_tcn()                                          /* (4.6.6)         */
{
   Int port_no;

   port_no = bridge_info.root_port;
   tcn_bpdu[port_no].type = Tcn_bpdu_type;

   send_tcn_bpdu(port_no, &tcn_bpdu[bridge_info.root_port]);/* (4.6.6.3)   */

}

      /* where

      send_tcn_bpdu(port_no,bpdu)
      Int         port_no;
      Tcn_bpdu    *bpdu;

      is a pseudo-implementation-specific routine which transmits
      the bpdu on the specified port within the specified time.

      */


configuration_update()                                  /* (4.6.7)         */
{
   root_selection();                                    /* (4.6.7.3.1)     */
                                                        /* (4.6.8.2)       */

   designated_port_selection();                         /* (4.6.7.3.2)     */
                                                        /* (4.6.9.2)       */
}
```

```
root_selection()                                        /* (4.6.8)      */
{
    Int root_port;
    Int port_no;

    root_port = No_port;

    for (port_no = One; port_no <= No_of_ports; port_no++)    /* (4.6.8.3.1) */
    {
        if ( ( (!designated_port(port_no))
                &&
                (port_info[port_no].state != Disabled)
                &&
                (port_info[port_no].designated_root < bridge_info.bridge_id)
            )
            &&
            ( (root_port == No_port)
                ||
                ( port_info[port_no].designated_root
                    < port_info[root_port].designated_root    /* (4.6.8.3.1(1)) */
                )
                ||
                ( ( port_info[port_no].designated_root
                    == port_info[root_port].designated_root
                    )
                    &&
                    ( ( ( port_info[port_no].designated_cost
                            + port_info[port_no].path_cost
                        )
                        <
                        ( port_info[root_port].designated_cost
                            + port_info[root_port].path_cost
                        )                                     /* (4.6.8.3.1(2)) */
                    )
                    ||
                    ( ( ( port_info[port_no].designated_cost
                            + port_info[port_no].path_cost
                        )
                        ==
                        ( port_info[root_port].designated_cost
                            + port_info[root_port].path_cost
                        )
                    )
                    &&
                    ( ( port_info[port_no].designated_bridge
                        < port_info[root_port].designated_bridge
                        )                                     /* (4.6.8.3.1(3)) */
                        ||
                        ( ( port_info[port_no].designated_bridge
                            == port_info[root_port].designated_bridge
                            )
                            &&
                            ( ( port_info[port_no].designated_port
                                < port_info[root_port].designated_port
                                )                             /* (4.6.8.3.1(4)) */
                                ||
                                ( ( port_info[port_no].designated_port
```

```
                              == port_info[root_port].designated_port
                    )
                    &&
                    (  port_info[port_no].port_id
                       <  port_info[root_port].port_id
                    )                          /* (4.6.8.3.1(5)) */
    ) ) ) ) ) ) ) ) )
    {
        root_port = port_no;
    }
}

bridge_info.root_port = root_port;              /* (4.6.8.3.1)    */

if (root_port == No_port)                       /* (4.6.8.3.2)    */
{

    bridge_info.designated_root = bridge_info.bridge_id;
                                                /* (4.6.8.3.2(1)) */
    bridge_info.root_path_cost = Zero;          /* (4.6.8.3.2(2)) */
}
else                                            /* (4.6.8.3.3)    */
{
    bridge_info.designated_root = port_info[root_port].designated_root;
                                                /* (4.6.8.3.3(1)) */
    bridge_info.root_path_cost = (  port_info[root_port].designated_cost
                            + port_info[root_port].path_cost
                    );                          /* (4.6.8.3.3(2)) */
}
}
```

```
designated_port_selection()                              /* (4.6.9)      */
{
   Int port_no;

   for (port_no = One; port_no <= No_of_ports; port_no++)  /* (4.6.9.3)    */
   {
      if (  designated_port(port_no)                      /* (4.6.9.3.1)  */
            ||
            (
               port_info[port_no].designated_root
               != bridge_info.designated_root             /* (4.6.9.3.2)  */
            )
            ||
            (  bridge_info.root_path_cost
               < port_info[port_no].designated_cost
            )                                              /* (4.6.9.3.3)  */
            ||
            (  (  bridge_info.root_path_cost
                  == port_info[port_no].designated_cost
               )
               &&
               (  (  bridge_info.bridge_id
                     < port_info[port_no].designated_bridge
                  )                                        /* (4.6.9.3.4)  */
                  ||
                  (  (  bridge_info.bridge_id
                           == port_info[port_no].designated_bridge
                     )
                     &&
                     (  port_info[port_no].port_id
                        <= port_info[port_no].designated_port
                     )                                     /* (4.6.9.3.5)  */
      ) ) ) )
      {
         become_designated_port(port_no);                 /* (4.6.10.2.2) */
      }
   }
}

become_designated_port(port_no)                           /* (4.6.10)     */
Int port_no;
{
   port_info[port_no].designated_root = bridge_info.designated_root;
                                                          /* (4.6.10.3.1) */

   port_info[port_no].designated_cost = bridge_info.root_path_cost;
                                                          /* (4.6.10.3.2) */

   port_info[port_no].designated_bridge = bridge_info.bridge_id;
                                                          /* (4.6.10.3.3) */

   port_info[port_no].designated_port = port_info[port_no].port_id;
                                                          /* (4.6.10.3.4) */
}
```

```
port_state_selection()                                /* (4.6.11)        */
{
    Int port_no;

    for (port_no = One; port_no <= No_of_ports; port_no++)
    {
        if (port_no == bridge_info.root_port)             /* (4.6.11.3.1)    */
        {
            port_info[port_no].config_pending = False;       /* (4.6.11.3.1(1))*/
            port_info[port_no].topology_change_acknowledge = False;

            make_forwarding(port_no);                     /* (4.6.11.3.1(2))*/
        }
        else if (designated_port(port_no))                /* (4.6.11.3.2)    */
        {
            stop_message_age_timer(port_no);              /* (4.6.11.3.2(1))*/

            make_forwarding(port_no);                     /* (4.6.11.3.2(2))*/
        }
        else                                              /* (4.6.11.3.3)    */
        {
            port_info[port_no].config_pending = False;       /* (4.6.11.3.3(1))*/
            port_info[port_no].topology_change_acknowledge = False;

            make_blocking(port_no);                       /* (4.6.11.3.3(2))*/
        }
    }
}
```

```
make_forwarding(port_no)                          /* (4.6.12)       */
Int port_no;
{
   if (port_info[port_no].state == Blocking)      /* (4.6.12.3)     */
   {
      set_port_state(port_no, Listening);         /* (4.6.12.3.1)   */

      start_forward_delay_timer(port_no);         /* (4.6.12.3.2)   */
   }
}



make_blocking(port_no)                            /* (4.6.13)       */
Int port_no;
{
   if (  (port_info[port_no].state != Disabled)
      &&
         (port_info[port_no].state != Blocking)
      )                                           /* (4.6.13.3)     */
   {
      if (  (port_info[port_no].state == Forwarding)
         ||
            (port_info[port_no].state == Learning)
         )
      {
         topology_change_detection();            /* (4.6.13.3.1)   */
                                                 /* (4.6.14.2.3)   */
      }

      set_port_state(port_no, Blocking);          /* (4.6.13.3.2)   */

      stop_forward_delay_timer(port_no);          /* (4.6.13.3.3)   */
   }
}

      /* where */

      set_port_state(port_no, state)
      Int port_no;
      State state;
      {
            port_info[port_no].state = state;
      }
```

```
topology_change_detection()                              /* (4.6.14)      */
{
   if (root_bridge())                                    /* (4.6.14.3.1)  */
   {
      bridge_info.topology_change = True;                /* (4.6.14.3.1(1))*/

      start_topology_change_timer();                     /* (4.6.14.3.1(2))*/
   }

   else if (bridge_info.topology_change_detected == False) /* (4.6.14.3.2)  */
   {
      transmit_tcn();                                    /* (4.6.14.3.2(1))*/

      start_tcn_timer();                                 /* (4.6.14.3.2(2))*/
   }

   bridge_info.topology_change_detected = True;          /* (4.6.14.3.3)  */
}


topology_change_acknowledged()                           /* (4.6.15)      */
{
   bridge_info.topology_change_detected = False;         /* (4.6.15.3.1)  */

   stop_tcn_timer();                                     /* (4.6.15.3.2)  */
}


acknowledge_topology_change(port_no)                     /* (4.6.16)      */
Int port_no;
{
   port_info[port_no].topology_change_acknowledge = True; /* (4.6.16.3.1)  */

   transmit_config(port_no);                             /* (4.6.16.3.2)  */
}
```

```
/** Operation of the Protocol (4.7) **/

received_config_bpdu(port_no, config)                        /* (4.7.1)        */
Int port_no;
Config_bpdu *config;
{
   Boolean root;

   root = root_bridge();

   if (port_info[port_no].state != Disabled)
   {
      if (supersedes_port_info(port_no, config))             /* (4.7.1.1)      */
      {                                                      /* (4.6.2.2)      */
         record_config_information(port_no, config);         /* (4.7.1.1.1)    */
                                                             /* (4.6.2.2)      */
         configuration_update();                             /* (4.7.1.1.2)    */
                                                             /* (4.6.7.2.1)    */
         port_state_selection();                             /* (4.7.1.1.3)    */
                                                             /* (4.6.11.2.1)   */

         if ((!root_bridge()) && root)                       /* (4.7.1.1.4)    */
         {
            stop_hello_timer();

            if (bridge_info.topology_change_detected)        /* (4.7.1.1.5)    */
            {
               stop_topology_change_timer();

               transmit_tcn();                               /* (4.6.6.1)      */

               start_tcn_timer();
            }
         }

         if (port_no == bridge_info.root_port)
         {
            record_config_timeout_values(config);            /* (4.7.1.1.6)    */
                                                             /* (4.6.3.2)      */
            config_bpdu_generation();                        /* (4.6.4.2.1)    */

            if (config->topology_change_acknowledgment)      /* (4.7.1.1.7)    */
            {
               topology_change_acknowledged();               /* (4.6.15.2)     */
            }
         }
      }

      else if (designated_port(port_no))                     /* (4.7.1.2)      */
      {
         reply(port_no);                                     /* (4.7.1.2.1)    */
                                                             /* (4.6.5.2)      */
      }
   }
}
```

```
received_tcn_bpdu(port_no, tcn)                              /* (4.7.2)        */
Int port_no;
Tcn_bpdu *tcn;
{
   if (port_info[port_no].state != Disabled)
   {
      if (designated_port(port_no))
      {
         topology_change_detection();                        /* (4.7.2.1)      */
                                                             /* (4.6.14.2.1)   */
         acknowledge_topology_change(port_no);               /* (4.7.2.2)      */
      }                                                       /* (4.6.16.2)     */
   }
}



hello_timer_expiry()                                          /* (4.7.3)        */
{
   config_bpdu_generation();                                 /* (4.6.4.2.2)    */

   start_hello_timer();
}
```

```
message_age_timer_expiry(port_no)                          /* (4.7.4)         */
Int port_no;
{
    Boolean root;

    root = root_bridge();

    become_designated_port(port_no);                       /* (4.7.4.1)       */
                                                           /* (4.6.10.2.1)    */
    configuration_update();                                /* (4.7.4.2)       */
                                                           /* (4.6.7.2.2)     */
    port_state_selection();                                /* (4.7.4.3)       */
                                                           /* (4.6.11.2.2)    */

    if ((root_bridge()) && (!root))                        /* (4.7.4.4)       */
    {
        bridge_info.max_age = bridge_info.bridge_max_age;      /* (4.7.4.4.1)   */
        bridge_info.hello_time = bridge_info.bridge_hello_time;
        bridge_info.forward_delay = bridge_info.bridge_forward_delay;

        topology_change_detection();                       /* (4.7.4.4.2)     */
                                                           /* (4.6.14.2.4)    */
        stop_tcn_timer();                                  /* (4.7.4.4.3)     */

        config_bpdu_generation();                          /* (4.7.4.4.4)     */
                                                           /* (4.6.4.4.3)     */
        start_hello_timer();
    }
}
```

```
forward_delay_timer_expiry(port_no)                      /* (4.7.5)     */
Int port_no;
{
   if (port_info[port_no].state == Listening)            /* (4.7.5.1)    */
   {
      set_port_state(port_no, Learning);                 /* (4.7.5.1.1)  */

      start_forward_delay_timer(port_no);                /* (4.7.5.1.2)  */
   }

   else if (port_info[port_no].state == Learning)        /* (4.7.5.2)    */
   {
      set_port_state(port_no, Forwarding);               /* (4.7.5.2.1)  */

      if (designated_for_some_port())                    /* (4.7.5.2.2)  */
      {
         topology_change_detection();                    /* (4.6.14.2.2) */
      }
   }
}


       /* where */

       Boolean designated_for_some_port()
       {
          Int port_no;

          for (port_no = One; port_no <= No_of_ports; port_no++)
          {
             if ( port_info[port_no].designated_bridge
                == bridge_info.bridge_id
                )
             {
                return(True);
             }
          }

          return(False);
       }
```

```
tcn_timer_expiry()                                    /* (4.7.6)       */
{
      transmit_tcn();                                 /* (4.7.6.1)     */

      start_tcn_timer();                              /* (4.7.6.2)     */
}


topology_change_timer_expiry()                        /* (4.7.7)       */
{
      bridge_info.topology_change_detected = False;   /* (4.7.7.1)     */

      bridge_info.topology_change = False;            /* (4.7.7.2)     */
}

hold_timer_expiry(port_no)                            /* (4.7.8)       */
Int port_no;
{
   if (port_info[port_no].config_pending)
   {
      transmit_config(port_no);                       /* (4.7.8.1)     */
   }                                                  /* (4.6.1.2.3)   */
}
```

```
/** Management of the Bridge Protocol Entity (4.8) **/
initialisation()                                          /* (4.8.1)        */
{
    Int port_no;

    bridge_info.designated_root = bridge_info.bridge_id;  /* (4.8.1.1)      */
    bridge_info.root_path_cost = Zero;
    bridge_info.root_port = No_port;

    bridge_info.max_age = bridge_info.bridge_max_age;     /* (4.8.1.2)      */
    bridge_info.hello_time = bridge_info.bridge_hello_time;
    bridge_info.forward_delay = bridge_info.bridge_forward_delay;

    bridge_info.topology_change_detected = False;         /* (4.8.1.3)      */
    bridge_info.topology_change = False;
    stop_tcn_timer();
    stop_topology_change_timer();

    for (port_no = One; port_no <= No_of_ports; port_no++) /* (4.8.1.4)     */
    {

        initialize_port(port_no);

    }

    port_state_selection();                              /* (4.8.1.5)      */

    config_bpdu_generation();                            /* (4.8.1.6)      */
    start_hello_timer();
}



    initialize_port(port_no)
    Int port_no;
    {

        become_designated_port(port_no);                 /* (4.8.1.4.1)    */

        set_port_state(port_no, Blocking);               /* (4.8.1.4.2)    */

        port_info[port_no].topology_change_acknowledge = False;
                                                         /* (4.8.1.4.3)    */

        port_info[port_no].config_pending = False;       /* (4.8.1.4.4)    */

        stop_message_age_timer(port_no);                 /* (4.8.1.4.5)    */

        stop_forward_delay_timer(port_no);               /* (4.8.1.4.6)    */

        stop_hold_timer(port_no);                        /* (4.8.1.4.7)    */
    }
```

```
enable_port(port_no)                                    /* (4.8.2)      */
Int port_no;
{

   initialize_port(port_no);

   port_state_selection();                              /* (4.8.2.7)    */
}




disable_port(port_no)                                   /* (4.8.3)      */
Int port_no;
{
   Boolean root;

   root = root_bridge();

   become_designated_port(port_no);                     /* (4.8.3.1)    */

   set_port_state(port_no, Disabled);                   /* (4.8.3.2)    */

   port_info[port_no].topology_change_acknowledge = False; /* (4.8.3.3)  */

   port_info[port_no].config_pending = False;           /* (4.8.3.4)    */

   stop_message_age_timer(port_no);                     /* (4.8.3.5)    */

   stop_forward_delay_timer(port_no);                   /* (4.8.3.6)    */

   configuration_update();

   port_state_selection();                              /* (4.8.3.7)    */

   if ((root_bridge()) && (!root))                      /* (4.8.3.8)    */
   {
      bridge_info.max_age = bridge_info.bridge_max_age;    /* (4.8.3.8.1) */
      bridge_info.hello_time = bridge_info.bridge_hello_time;
      bridge_info.forward_delay = bridge_info.bridge_forward_delay;

      topology_change_detection();                      /* (4.8.3.8.2)  */

      stop_tcn_timer();                                 /* (4.8.3.8.3)  */

      config_bpdu_generation();                         /* (4.8.3.8.4)  */

      start_hello_timer();
   }
}
```

```
set_bridge_priority(new_bridge_id)                    /* (4.8.4)      */
Identifier new_bridge_id;                             /* (4.8.4.1)    */
{
    Boolean root;
    Int port_no;

    root = root_bridge();

    for (port_no = One; port_no <= No_of_ports; port_no++)  /* (4.8.4.2)   */
    {
        if (designated_port(port_no))
        {
            port_info[port_no].designated_bridge = new_bridge_id;
        }
    }

    bridge_info.bridge_id = new_bridge_id;               /* (4.8.4.3)    */

    configuration_update();                              /* (4.8.4.4)    */

    port_state_selection();                             /* (4.8.4.5)    */

    if ((root_bridge()) && (!root))                     /* (4.8.4.6)    */
    {
        bridge_info.max_age = bridge_info.bridge_max_age;    /* (4.8.4.6.1) */
        bridge_info.hello_time = bridge_info.bridge_hello_time;
        bridge_info.forward_delay = bridge_info.bridge_forward_delay;

        topology_change_detection();                    /* (4.8.4.6.2)  */

        stop_tcn_timer();                               /* (4.8.4.6.3)  */

        config_bpdu_generation();                       /* (4.8.4.6.4)  */

        start_hello_timer();
    }
}
```

```
set_port_priority(port_no, new_port_id)              /* (4.8.5)      */
Int port_no;
Port_id new_port_id;                                 /* (4.8.5.1)    */
{
   if (designated_port(port_no))                     /* (4.8.5.2)    */
   {
      port_info[port_no].designated_port = new_port_id;
   }

   port_info[port_no].port_id = new_port_id;         /* (4.8.5.3)    */

   if ( (   bridge_info.bridge_id                    /* (4.8.5.4)    */
         == port_info[port_no].designated_bridge
        )
        &&
        (  port_info[port_no].port_id
           <  port_info[port_no].designated_port
        )
      )
   {
      become_designated_port(port_no);               /* (4.8.5.4.1)  */

      port_state_selection();                        /* (4.8.5.4.2)  */
   }
}



set_path_cost(port_no, path_cost)                    /* (4.8.6)      */
Int port_no;
Cost path_cost;
{
   port_info[port_no].path_cost = path_cost;         /* (4.8.6.1)    */

   configuration_update();                           /* (4.8.6.2)    */

   port_state_selection();                           /* (4.8.6.3)    */
}
```

```
/** pseudo-implementation-specific timer running support **/

tick()
{
   Int port_no;

   if (hello_timer_expired())
   { hello_timer_expiry();
   }

   if (tcn_timer_expired())
   { tcn_timer_expiry();
   }

   if (topology_change_timer_expired())
   { topology_change_timer_expiry();
   }

   for (port_no = One; port_no <= No_of_ports; port_no++)
   {
      if (forward_delay_timer_expired(port_no))
      {
         forward_delay_timer_expiry(port_no);
      }
      if (message_age_timer_expired(port_no))
      {
         message_age_timer_expiry(port_no);
      }
      if (hold_timer_expired(port_no))
      {
         hold_timer_expiry(port_no);
      }
   }
}

/* where */

start_hello_timer()
{ hello_timer.value = (Time) Zero;
   hello_timer.active = True;
}

stop_hello_timer()
{ hello_timer.active = False;
}

Boolean hello_timer_expired()
{ if (hello_timer.active && (++hello_timer.value >= bridge_info.hello_time))
   { hello_timer.active = False;
      return(True);
   }
   return(False);
}

start_tcn_timer()
{ tcn_timer.value = (Time) Zero;
   tcn_timer.active = True;
```

104

```
}

stop_tcn_timer()
{  tcn_timer.active = False;
}

Boolean tcn_timer_expired()
{  if (tcn_timer.active && (++tcn_timer.value >= bridge_info.bridge_hello_time))
    {   tcn_timer.active = False;
        return(True);
    }
    return(False);
}

start_topology_change_timer()
{  topology_change_timer.value = (Time) Zero;
    topology_change_timer.active = True;
}

stop_topology_change_timer()
{  topology_change_timer.active = False;
}

Boolean topology_change_timer_expired()
{  if ( topology_change_timer.active
        && ( ++topology_change_timer.value
            >= bridge_info.topology_change_time
          )
      )
    {   topology_change_timer.active = False;
        return(True);
    }
    return(False);
}

start_message_age_timer(port_no, message_age)
Int   port_no;
Time message_age;
{  message_age_timer[port_no].value = message_age;
    message_age_timer[port_no].active = True;
}

stop_message_age_timer(port_no)
Int   port_no;
{  message_age_timer[port_no].active = False;
}

Boolean message_age_timer_expired(port_no)
Int port_no;
{  if (message_age_timer[port_no].active &&
        (++message_age_timer[port_no].value >= bridge_info.max_age))
    {  message_age_timer[port_no].active = False;
        return(True);
    }
        return(False);
}
```

```
start_forward_delay_timer(port_no)
Int port_no;
{  forward_delay_timer[port_no].value = Zero;
   forward_delay_timer[port_no].active = True;
}


stop_forward_delay_timer(port_no)
Int port_no;
{  forward_delay_timer[port_no].active = False;
}


Boolean forward_delay_timer_expired(port_no)
Int port_no;
{  if (forward_delay_timer[port_no].active &&
       (++forward_delay_timer[port_no].value >= bridge_info.forward_delay))
   {   forward_delay_timer[port_no].active = False;
       return(True);
   }
   return(False);
}


start_hold_timer(port_no)
Int port_no;
{  hold_timer[port_no].value = Zero;
   hold_timer[port_no].active = True;
}


stop_hold_timer(port_no)
Int port_no;
{  hold_timer[port_no].active = False;
}


Boolean hold_timer_expired(port_no)
Int port_no;
{  if (hold_timer[port_no].active &&
       (++hold_timer[port_no].value >= bridge_info.hold_time))
   {   hold_timer[port_no].active = False;
       return(True);
   }
   return(False);
}


/** pseudo-implementation-specific transmit routines **/

#include "transmit.c"
```

4.10 Performance. This section places requirements on the performance of the Bridges in a Bridged Local Area Network and on the setting of the parameters of the Spanning Tree Algorithm and Protocol. These are necessary to ensure that the algorithm and protocol operate correctly.

It recommends default operational values for performance parameters. These have been specified in order to avoid the need to set values prior to operation, and have been chosen with a view to maximizing the ease with which Bridged Local Area Network components interoperate.

It specifies absolute maximum values for performance parameters. The ranges of applicable values are specified to assist in the choice of operational values and to provide guidance to implementors.

4.10.1 Requirements. For correct operation, the parameters and configuration of Bridges in the Bridged Local Area Network ensure that

(1) Bridges do not initiate reconfiguration if none is needed. This means that a Bridge Protocol Message is not timed out before its successor arrives, unless a failure has occurred.

(2) Following reconfiguration frames are not forwarded on the new active topology, while frames that were initially forwarded on the previous active topology are still in the Bridged Local Area Network. This ensures that frames are not duplicated.

These requirements are met through placing restrictions on

(a) The **maximum bridge diameter** of the Bridge Local Area Network, the maximum number of Bridges between any two points of attachment of end stations.

(b) The **maximum bridge transit delay**, the maximum time elapsing between reception and transmission by a Bridge of a forwarded frame, frames that would otherwise exceed this limit being discarded.

(c) The **maximum BPDU transmission delay**, the maximum delay prior to the transmission of a Bridge Protocol Data Unit following the need to transmit such a BPDU arising, as specified in 4.7.

(d) The **maximum Message Age increment overestimate** that may be made to the value of the Message Age parameter in transmitted BPDUs or to the age of stored Bridge Protocol Message information.

(e) The values of the **Bridge Hello Time**, **Bridge Max Age**, **Bridge Forward Delay**, and **Hold Time** parameters.

Additionally a Bridge shall not

(i) Underestimate the increment to the Message Age parameter in transmitted BPDUs.

(ii) Underestimate Forward Delay.

(iii) Overestimate the Hello Time interval when acting as the Root.

4.10.2 Parameter Values. Recommended default, absolute maximum, and ranges of parameters are specified in Tables 4-1, 4-2, 4-3, 4-4, and 4-5.

A Bridge shall not exceed the absolute maximum values specified in Table 4-2 for **maximum bridge transit delay**, **maximum BPDU transmission delay** and **maximum Message Age increment overestimate**.

Table 4-1
Maximum Bridge Diameter

Parameter	Recommended Value
maximum bridge diameter	7

Table 4-2
Transit and Transmission Delays

Parameter	Recommended Value	Absolute Maximum
maximum bridge transit delay	1.0	4.0
maximum BPDU transmission delay	1.0	4.0
maximum Message Age increment overestimate	1.0	4.0

All times are in seconds.

Table 4-3
Spanning Tree Algorithm Timer Values

Parameter	Recommended or Default Value	Fixed Value	Range	
Bridge Hello Time	2.0	—	1.0	– 10.0
Bridge Max Age	20.0	—	6.0	– 40.0
Bridge Forward Delay	15.0	—	4.0	– 30.0
Hold Time	—	1.0	—	

All times are in seconds.
— Not applicable.
4.10.2 constrains the relationship between Bridge Max Age and Bridge Forward Delay.

Table 4-4
Bridge and Port Priority Parameter Values

Parameter	Recommended or Default Value	Range	
Bridge Priority	32768	0 –	65535
Port Priority	128	0 –	255

Table 4-5
Path Cost Parameter Values

Parameter	Recommended Value	Absolute Minimum	Range	
Path Cost	see 4.10.2	1	1 –	65535

If the values of **Bridge Hello Time**, **Bridge Max Age**, and **Bridge Forward Delay** can be set by management, the Bridge shall have the capability to use the full range of values in the parameter ranges specified in Table 4-3, with a granularity of 1 second.

A Bridge shall use the value of **Hold Time** shown in Table 4-3.

A Bridge shall enforce the following relationships:

$$2 \times (Bridge\_Forward\_Delay - 1.0\ seconds) \geq Bridge\_Max\_Age$$

$$Bridge\_Max\_Age \geq 2 \times (Bridge\_Hello\_Time + 1.0\ seconds)$$

It is recommended that default values of the **Path Cost** parameter for each Bridge Port be based on the following formula:

$$Path\_Cost = 1000/Attached\_LAN\_speed\_in\_Mb/s$$

which gives a default value for **Path Cost** of 100 for a 10 Mb/s LAN.

If the values of the **Bridge Priority** and the **Port Priority** for each of the Ports can be set by management, the Bridge shall have the capability to use the full range of values in the parameter ranges specified in Table 4-4, with a granularity of 1.

A Bridge shall not use a lower value for the **Path Cost** parameter associated with any Port than the absolute minimum value specified in Table 4-5.

If the value of **Path Cost** can be set by management, the Bridge shall have the capability to use the full range of values in the parameter ranges specified in Table 4-5, with a granularity of 1.

5. Encoding of Bridge Protocol Data Units

This section specifies the structure and encoding of the Bridge Protocol Data Units (BPDUs) exchanged between Bridge Protocol Entities.

5.1 Structure

5.1.1 Transmission and Representation of Octets. All BPDUs shall contain an integral number of octets. The octets in a BPDU are numbered starting from 1 and increasing in the order they are put into a Data Link Service Data Unit (DLSDU). The bits in an octet are numbered from 1 to 8, where 1 is the low-order bit.

When consecutive octets are used to represent a binary number, the lower octet number has the most significant value.

All Bridge Protocol Entities respect these bit and octet ordering conventions, thus allowing communications to take place.

When the encoding of a BPDU is represented using a diagram in this section, the following representation is used:

(1) Octets are shown with the lowest numbered octet to the left, higher numbered octets being to the right.

(2) Within an octet, bits are shown with bit 8 to the left and bit 1 to the right.

5.1.2 Components. A Protocol Identifier is encoded in the initial octets of all BPDUs. This standard reserves a single Protocol Identifier value. This standard places no further restriction on the structure, encoding, or use of BPDUs with different values of the Protocol Identifier field, should these exist, by other standard protocols.

BPDUs used by Bridge Protocol Entities operating the Spanning Tree Algorithm and Protocol specified in Section 4 use the reserved Protocol Identifier value and have the following structure.

Each BPDU comprises a fixed number of parameters essential to the operation of the protocol. Each parameter is encoded in one or more octets and is of fixed length. The order of parameters in a BPDU is fixed.

The parameters of each BPDU are determined by the BPDU type; all BPDUs of the same type shall comprise the same parameters, in the same order, encoded in the same way.

5.2 Encoding of Parameter Types

5.2.1 Encoding of Protocol Identifiers. A Protocol Identifier shall be encoded in two octets.

5.2.2 Encoding of Protocol Version Identifiers. A Protocol Version Identifier shall be encoded in one octet. If two Protocol Version Identifiers are interpreted as unsigned binary numbers, then the greater number will be associated with the more recently defined Protocol Version.

5.2.3 Encoding of BPDU Types. The type of the BPDU shall be encoded as a single octet. The bit pattern contained in the octet merely serves to distinguish the type; no ordering relationship between BPDUs of different types is implied.

5.2.4 Encoding of Flags. A flag shall be encoded as a bit in a single octet. A number of flags may be thus encoded in a single octet. A flag is set if the corresponding bit in the octet takes the value 1. Bit positions in the octet that do not correspond to flags defined for a given type of BPDU are reset, i.e., shall take the value 0. No additional flags will be defined for a BPDU of given protocol version and type.

5.2.5 Encoding of Bridge Identifiers. A Bridge Identifier shall be encoded as eight octets, taken to represent an unsigned binary number. Two Bridge Identifiers may be numerically compared, the lesser number shall denote the Bridge of the higher priority.

The two most significant octets of a Bridge Identifier comprise a settable priority component that permits the relative priority of Bridges to be managed (4.5.3.7, Section 6). The six least significant octets ensure the uniqueness of the Bridge Identifier; they shall be derived from the globally unique Bridge Address (3.12.5) according to the following procedure.

The third most significant octet is derived from the initial octet of the MAC address, the least significant bit of the octet (Bit 1) is assigned the value of the first bit of the Bridge Address, the next most significant bit, the value of the second bit of the Bridge Address, and so on. In a Bridged Local Area Network utilizing 48-bit MAC addresses, the fourth through eighth octets are similarly assigned the values of the second to the sixth octets of the Bridge Address.

In a Bridged Local Area Network utilizing 16-bit MAC addresses, the fourth octet is assigned the value of the second octet of the Bridge Address, and the fifth through eighth octets are assigned the value 0000 0000.

5.2.6 Encoding of Root Path Cost. Root Path Cost shall be encoded as four octets, taken to represent an unsigned binary number, a multiple of arbitrary cost units. Subsection 4.10.2 contains recommendations as to the increment to the Root Path Cost, in order that some common value can be placed on this parameter without requiring a management installation practice for Bridges in a Bridged Local Area Network.

5.2.7 Encoding of Port Identifiers. A Port Identifier shall be encoded as two octets, taken to represent an unsigned binary number. If two Port Identifiers are numerically compared, the lesser number shall denote the Port of higher priority. The more significant octet of a Port Identifier is a settable priority component that permits the relative priority of Ports on the same Bridge to be managed (4.5.5, Section 6). The less significant octet is the Port Number expressed as an unsigned binary number. The value 0 is not used as a Port Number.

5.2.8 Encoding of Timer Values. Timer Values shall be encoded in two octets, taken to represent an unsigned binary number multiplied by a unit of time of

1/256 of a second. This permits times in the range 0 to, but not including, 256 seconds to be represented.

5.3 BPDU Formats and Parameters

5.3.1 Configuration BPDUs. The format of the Configuration BPDUs is shown in Fig 5-1. Each transmitted Configuration BPDU shall contain the following parameters (4.5.1) and no others:

   (1) The Protocol Identifier is encoded in Octets 1 and 2 of the BPDU. It takes the value 0000 0000 0000 0000, which identifies the Spanning Tree Algorithm and Protocol as specified in Section 4 of this standard.
   (2) The Protocol Version Identifier is encoded in Octet 3 of the BPDU. It takes the value 0000 0000.
   (3) The BPDU Type is encoded in Octet 4 of the BPDU. This field shall take the value 0000 0000. This denotes a Configuration BPDU.
   (4) The Topology Change Acknowledgment flag is encoded in Bit 8 of Octet 5 of the BPDU.
   (5) The Topology Change flag is encoded in Bit 1 of Octet 5 of the BPDU.
   (6) The Root Identifier is encoded in Octets 6 through 13 of the BPDU.
   (7) The Root Path Cost is encoded in Octets 14 through 17 of the BPDU.
   (8) The Bridge Identifier is encoded in Octets 18 through 25 of the BPDU.
   (9) The Port Identifier is encoded in Octets 26 and 27 of the BPDU.
   (10) The Message Age timer value is encoded in Octets 28 and 29 of the BPDU.
   (11) The Max Age timer value is encoded in Octets 30 and 31 of the BPDU.
   (12) The Hello Time timer value is encoded in Octets 32 and 33 of the BPDU.
   (13) The Forward Delay timer value is encoded in Octets 34 and 35 of the BPDU.

5.3.2 Topology Change Notification BPDUs. The format of the Topology Change Notification BPDUs is shown in Fig 5-2. Each transmitted Topology Change Notification BPDU shall contain the following parameters (4.5.2) and no others:

   (1) The Protocol Identifier is encoded in Octets 1 and 2 of the BPDU. It takes the value 0000 0000 0000 0000, which identifies the Spanning Tree Algorithm and Protocol as specified in Section 4 of this standard.
   (2) The Protocol Version Identifier is encoded in Octet 3 of the BPDU. It takes the value 0000 0000.
   (3) The BPDU Type is encoded in Octet 4 of the BPDU. This field shall take the value 1000 0000. This denotes a Topology Change Notification BPDU.

5.3.3 Validation of Received BPDUs. A received BPDU shall be processed by the Bridge Protocol Entity as specified in 4.7 of this standard if, and only if, it contains the Protocol Identifier, Protocol Version Identifier, and BPDU Type parameters, and either

   (1) The BPDU Type parameter denotes a Configuration BPDU, and all of the fixed parameters of this BPDU type are present, i.e., the BPDU is composed of at least 35 octets, or
   (2) The BPDU Type parameter denotes a Topology Change Notification BPDU, and all of the fixed parameters of this BPDU type are present, i.e., the BPDU is composed of at least 4 octets.

Field	Octet
Protocol Identifier	1
	2
Protocol Version Identifier	3
BPDU Type	4
Flags	5
Root Identifier	6
	7
	8
	9
	10
	11
	12
	13
Root Path Cost	14
	15
	16
	17
Bridge Identifier	18
	19
	20
	21
	22
	23
	24
	25
Port Identifier	26
	27
Message Age	28
	29
Max Age	30
	31
Hello Time	32
	33
Forward Delay	34
	35.

Fig 5-1
Configuration BPDU Parameters and Format

	Octet
Protocol Identifier	1 2
Protocol Version Identifier	3
BPDU Type	4

Fig 5-2
Topology Change Notification BPDU Parameters and Format

6. Bridge Management

Management facilities are provided by MAC Bridges in accordance with the principles and concepts of the OSI Management Framework.

This section

(1) Introduces the Functional Areas of OSI Management to assist in the identification of the requirements placed on Bridges for the support of management facilities.

(2) Establishes the correspondence between the Processes used to model the operation of the Bridge (3.3) and the managed objects of the Bridge.

(3) Specifies the management operations supported by each managed object.

6.1 Management Functions. The Functions of Management relate to the users' needs for facilities that support the planning, organization, supervision, control, protection, and security of communications resources, and account for their use. These facilities may be categorized as supporting the Functional Areas of Configuration, Fault, Performance, Security, and Accounting Management. Each of these is summarized in 6.1.1 through 6.1.5, together with the facilities commonly required for the management of communication resources, and the particular facilities provided in that functional area by Bridge Management.

6.1.1 Configuration Management. Configuration Management provides for the identification of communications resources, initialization, reset and closedown, the supply of operational parameters, and the establishment and discovery of the relationship between resources. The facilities provided by Bridge Management in this functional area are

(1) The identification of all Bridges that together make up the Bridged Local Area Network and their respective locations and, as a consequence of that identification, the location of specific end stations to particular individual LANs.

(2) The ability to remotely reset, i.e., reinitialize, specified Bridges.

(3) The ability to control the priority with which a Bridge Port transmits frames.

(4) The ability to force a specific configuration of the spanning tree.

(5) The ability to control the propagation of frames with specific group MAC addresses to certain parts of the configured Bridged Local Area Network.

6.1.2 Fault Management. Fault Management provides for fault prevention, detection, diagnosis, and correction. The facilities provided by Bridge Management in this functional area are

(1) The ability to identify and correct Bridge malfunctions, including error logging and reporting.

6.1.3 Performance Management. Performance management provides for evaluation of the behavior of communications resources and of the effectiveness of communication activities. The facilities provided by Bridge Management in this functional area are

(1) The ability to gather statistics relating to performance and traffic analysis. Specific metrics include network utilization, frame forward, and frame discard counts for individual Ports within a Bridge.

6.1.4 Security Management. Security Management provides for the protection of resources. Bridge Management does not provide any specific facilities in this functional area.

6.1.5 Accounting Management. Accounting Management provides for the identification and distribution of costs and the setting of charges. Bridge Management does not provide any specific facilities in this functional area.

6.2 Managed Objects. Managed objects model the semantics of management operations. Operations upon an object supply information concerning, or facilitate control over, the Process or Entity associated with that object.

The managed resources of a MAC Bridge are those of the Processes and Entities established in 3.3 Model of Operation. Specifically,

(1) The Bridge Management Entity (6.4, 3.11).
(2) The individual Media Access Control Entities associated with each Bridge Port (6.5, 3.2, 3.5, 3.6).
(3) The Forwarding Process of the MAC Relay Entity (6.6, 3.2, 3.7).
(4) The Filtering Database of the MAC Relay Entity (6.7, 3.9).
(5) The Bridge Protocol Entity (6.8, 3.10, Section 4).

The management of each of these resources is described in terms of managed objects and operations below.

6.3 Data Types. This section specifies the semantics of operations independent of their encoding in management protocol. The data types of the parameters of operations are defined only as required for that specification.

The following data types are used:

(1) Boolean.
(2) Enumerated, for a collection of named values.
(3) Unsigned, for all parameters specified as "the number of" some quantity, and for priority values that are numerically compared. In the latter case the lower number represents the higher priority value.
(4) MAC Address.
(5) Latin1 String, as defined by ANSI X3.159 [1], for all text strings.
(6) Time Interval, an Unsigned value representing a positive integral number of seconds, for all protocol timeout parameters.
(7) Counter, for all parameters specified as a "count" of some quantity. A counter increments and wraps with a modulus of 2 to the power of 64.

6.4 Bridge Management Entity. The Bridge Management Entity is described in 3.11.

The objects which comprise this managed resource are

(1) The Bridge Configuration.

(2) The Port Configuration for each Port.

6.4.1 Bridge Configuration. The Bridge Configuration object models the operations that modify, or enquire about, the configuration of the Bridge's resources. There is a single Bridge Configuration object per Bridge.

The management operations that can be performed on the Bridge Configuration are Discover Bridge, Read Bridge, Set Bridge Name, and Reset Bridge.

6.4.1.1 Discover Bridge

6.4.1.1.1 Purpose. To solicit configuration information regarding the Bridge(s) in the Bridged Local Area Network.

6.4.1.1.2 Inputs

(1) Inclusion Range, a set of ordered pairs of specific MAC Addresses. Each pair specifies a range of MAC Addresses. A Bridge shall respond if and only if

  (a) For one of the pairs, the numerical comparison of its Bridge Address with each MAC Address of the pair shows it to be greater than or equal to the first, and

  (b) Less than or equal to the second, and

  (c) Its Bridge Address does not appear in the Exclusion List parameter below.

  The numerical comparison of one MAC Address with another, for the purpose of this operation, is achieved by deriving a number from the MAC Address according to the following procedure. The consecutive octets of the MAC Address are taken to represent a binary number; the first octet that would be transmitted on a LAN medium when the MAC Address is used in the source or destination fields of a MAC frame has the most significant value, the next octet the next most significant value. Within each octet the first bit of each octet is the least significant bit.

(2) Exclusion List, a list of specific MAC addresses.

6.4.1.1.3 Outputs

(1) Bridge Address—the MAC Address for the Bridge from which the Bridge Identifier used by the Spanning Tree Algorithm and Protocol is derived.

(2) Bridge Name—a text string of up to 32 characters, of locally determined significance.

(3) Number of Ports—the number of Bridge Ports (MAC Entities).

(4) Port Addresses—a list specifying the following for each Port:

  (a) Port Number—the number of the Bridge Port.

  (b) Port Address—the specific MAC Address of the individual MAC Entity associated with the Port.

(5) Uptime—count in seconds of the time elapsed since the Bridge was last reset or initialized.

6.4.1.2 Read Bridge

6.4.1.2.1 Purpose. To obtain general information regarding the Bridge.

6.4.1.2.2 Inputs. None.

6.4.1.2.3 Outputs

(1) Bridge Address—the MAC Address for the Bridge from which the Bridge Identifier used by the Spanning Tree Algorithm and Protocol is derived.
(2) Bridge Name—a text string of up to 32 characters, of locally determined significance.
(3) Number of Ports—the number of Bridge Ports (MAC Entities).
(4) Port Addresses—a list specifying the following for each Port:
    (a) Port Number.
    (b) Port Address—the specific MAC Address of the individual MAC Entity associated with the Port.
(5) Uptime—count in seconds of the time elapsed since the Bridge was last reset or initialized.

6.4.1.3 Set Bridge Name

6.4.1.3.1 Purpose. To associate a text string, readable by the Read Bridge operation, with a Bridge.

6.4.1.3.2 Inputs

(1) Bridge Name—a text string of up to 32 characters.

6.4.1.3.3 Outputs. None.

6.4.1.4 Reset Bridge

6.4.1.4.1 Purpose. To reset the specified Bridge. The Forwarding Database is cleared and initialized with the entries specified in the Permanent Database, and the Bridge Protocol Entity is initialized (4.8.1).

6.4.1.4.2 Inputs. None.

6.4.1.4.3 Outputs. None.

6.4.2 Port Configuration.

The Port Configuration object models the operations which modify, or inquire about, the configuration of the Ports of a Bridge. There are a fixed set of Bridge Ports per Bridge (one for each MAC interface), and each is identified by a permanently allocated Port Number. Ports are numbered consecutively starting from 1.

The information provided by the Port Configuration consists of summary data indicating its state and type. Specific counter information pertaining to the number of packets forwarded, filtered, and errors are maintained by the Forwarding Process resource. The management operations supported by Bridge Protocol Entity allows for controlling the states of each Port.

The management operations that can be performed on the Port Entities are Read Port and Set Port Name.

6.4.2.1 Read Port

6.4.2.1.1 Purpose. To obtain general information regarding a specific Bridge Port.

6.4.2.1.2 Inputs

(1) Port Number—the number of the Bridge Port.

6.4.2.1.3 Outputs

(1) Port Name—a text string of up to 32 characters, of locally determined significance.
(2) Port Type—the MAC Entity type of the Port (ISO/IEC 8802-3 [5]; ISO/IEC 8802-4 [6]; IEEE Std 802.5 [7]; other).

6.4.2.2 Set Port Name

6.4.2.2.1 Purpose. To associate a text string, readable by the Read Port operation, with a Bridge Port.

6.4.2.2.2 Inputs

(1) Port Number.

(2) Port Name — a text string of up to 32 characters.

6.4.2.2.3 Outputs. None.

6.5 Media Access Control Entities.
The Management Operations and Facilities provided by the MAC Entities are those specified in the Layer Management Standards of the individual MACs. A MAC Entity is associated with each Bridge Port.

6.6 Forwarding Process.
The Forwarding Process contains information relating to the forwarding of frames. Counters are maintained that provide information on the number of frames forwarded, filtered, and dropped due to error. Configuration data, defining how frame priority is handled, is maintained by the Forwarding Process.

The objects that comprise this managed resource are

(1) The Port Counters.

(2) The Transmission Priority objects for each Port.

6.6.1 The Port Counters. The Port Counters object models the operations that can be performed on the Port counters of the Forwarding Process resource. There are multiple instances (one for each MAC Entity) of the Port Counters object per Bridge.

The management operation that can be performed on the Port Counters is Read Forwarding Port Counters.

6.6.1.1 Read Forwarding Port Counters

6.6.1.1.1 Purpose. To read the forwarding counters associated with a specific Bridge Port.

6.6.1.1.2 Inputs

(1) Port Number.

6.6.1.1.3 Outputs

(1) Frames Received — count of valid frames received.

(2) Discard Inbound — count of valid frames received that were discarded by the Forwarding Process.

(3) Forward Outbound — count of frames forwarded to the associated MAC Entity.

(4) Discard Lack of Buffers — count of frames that were to be transmitted through the associated Port but were discarded due to lack of buffers.

(5) Discard Transit Delay Exceeded — count of frames that were to be transmitted but were discarded due to the maximum bridge transit delay being exceeded (buffering may have been available).

(6) Discard on Error — count of frames that were to be forwarded on the associated MAC but could not be transmitted (e.g., frame would be too large).

(7) Discard on Error Details — a list of 16 elements, each containing the source address of a frame and the reason why the frame was discarded (frame too

large). The list is maintained as a circular buffer. The only reason for discard on error, at present, is transmissible service data unit size exceeded.

6.6.2 Transmission Priority. The Transmission Priority object models the operations that can be performed to control how frame priority is handled for each transmitting Port, in accordance with 3.7.4. There are multiple instances (one for each MAC Entity) of the Transmission Priority objects per Bridge.

The management operations that can be performed on the Transmission Priority are Read Transmission Priority and Set Transmission Priority.

6.6.2.1 Read Transmission Priority

6.6.2.1.1 Purpose. To read the settings of the parameters governing the use of priority for relayed frames.

6.6.2.1.2 Inputs

(1) Port Number.

6.6.2.1.3 Outputs

(1) Outbound User Priority, in the range 0 through 7.
(2) Outbound Access Priority, in the range 0 through 7.

6.6.2.2 Set Transmission Priority

6.6.2.2.1 Purpose. To set the parameters governing the use of priority for relayed frames.

6.6.2.2.2 Inputs

(1) Port Number.
(2) Outbound User Priority, in the range 0 through 7.
(3) Outbound Access Priority, in the range 0 through 7.

6.6.2.2.3 Outputs. None.

6.7 Filtering Database. The Filtering Database is described in 3.9. It contains filtering information used by the Forwarding Process (3.7) in deciding through which Ports of the Bridge frames should be forwarded.

The objects that comprise this managed resource are

(1) The Filtering Database
(2) The Static Entries
(3) The Dynamic Entries
(4) The Permanent Database

6.7.1 The Filtering Database. The Filtering Database object models the operations that can be performed on, or affect, the Filtering Database as a whole. There is a single Filtering Database object per Bridge.

The management operations that can be performed on the Database are Read Filtering Database, Set Filtering Database Ageing Time, and the Create Filtering Entry, Delete Filtering Entry, Read Filtering Entry, and Read Filtering Entry Range operations defined in 6.7.5.

6.7.1.1 Read Filtering Database

6.7.1.1.1 Purpose. To obtain general information regarding the Bridge's Filtering Database.

6.7.1.1.2 Inputs. None.

6.7.1.1.3 Outputs

(1) Filtering Database Size — the maximum number of entries that can be held in the Filtering Database.
(2) Number of Static Entries — the number of static entries currently in the Filtering Database.
(3) Number of Dynamic Entries — the number of dynamic entries currently in the Filtering Database.
(4) Ageing Time — for ageing out dynamic entries when the Port associated with the entry is in the Forwarding State.

6.7.1.2 Set Filtering Database Ageing Time

6.7.1.2.1 Purpose. To set the ageing time for dynamic entries.

6.7.1.2.2 Inputs

(1) Ageing Time.

6.7.1.2.3 Outputs. None.

6.7.2 A Static Entry. A Static Entry object models the operations that can be performed on a single static entry in the Filtering Database. The set of Static Entry objects within the Filtering Database changes under management control.

A Static Entry object supports the Create Filtering Entry, Delete Filtering Entry, and Read Filtering Entry operations defined in 6.7.5.

6.7.3 A Dynamic Entry. A Dynamic Entry object models the operations that can be performed on a single dynamic entry (i.e., one that is created by the Learning Process as a result of the observation of network traffic) in the Filtering Database.

A Dynamic Entry object supports the Delete Filtering Entry and Read Filtering Entry operations defined in 6.7.5.

6.7.4 Permanent Database. The Permanent Database object models the operations that can be performed on, or affect, the Permanent Database. There is a single Permanent Database per Filtering Database.

The management operations that can be performed on the Permanent Database are Read Permanent Database, and the Create Filtering Entry, Delete Filtering Entry, Read Filtering Entry, and Read Filtering Entry Range operations defined in 6.7.5.

6.7.4.1 Read Permanent Database

6.7.4.1.1 Purpose. To obtain general information regarding the Permanent Database.

6.7.4.1.2 Inputs. None.

6.7.4.1.3 Outputs

(1) Permanent Database Size — maximum number of entries that can be held in the Permanent Database.
(2) Number of Permanent Entries — number of entries currently in the Permanent Database.

6.7.5 General Filtering Database Operations

6.7.5.1 Create Filtering Entry

6.7.5.1.1 Purpose. To create an entry in the Filtering Database or Permanent Database. Only Static Entries may be created in the Filtering Database.

6.7.5.1.2 Inputs

(1) Identifier — Filtering Database or Permanent Database.
(2) Address — MAC address of the entry.

(3) Port Map—a list specifying the following for each Port:
    (a) Inbound Port—the number of the Bridge Port.
    (b) Outbound Ports—a set of Boolean indicators, one for each Bridge Port.
If a member of Outbound Ports is True, the entry permits forwarding to the associated Port. The member of Outbound Ports that represents the Inbound Port takes the value False.

6.7.5.1.3 Outputs. None.

6.7.5.2 Delete Filtering Entry

6.7.5.2.1 Purpose. To delete an entry from the Filtering Database or Permanent Database.

6.7.5.2.2 Inputs

(1) Identifier—Filtering Database or Permanent Database.
(2) Address—MAC address of the desired entry.

6.7.5.2.3 Outputs. None.

6.7.5.3 Read Filtering Entry

6.7.5.3.1 Purpose. To read an entry from the Filtering or Permanent Databases.

6.7.5.3.2 Inputs

(1) Identifier—Filtering Database or Permanent Database.
(2) Address—MAC address of the desired entry.

6.7.5.3.3 Outputs

(1) Address—MAC address of the desired entry.
(2) Entry Type—either Dynamic or Static.
(3) Either
    (a) Port Number, if the Entry Type is Dynamic, or
    (b) Port Map, as specified for the Create Static Entry operation, if the Entry Type is Static.

6.7.5.4 Read Filtering Entry Range

6.7.5.4.1 Purpose. To read a range of entries from the Filtering or Permanent Databases.

Since the number of values to be returned in the requested range may have exceeded the capacity of the service data unit conveying the management response, the returned entry range is identified. The indices that define the range take on values from zero up to Filtering Database Size minus one.

6.7.5.4.2 Inputs

(1) Identifier—Filtering Database or Permanent Database.
(2) Start Index—inclusive starting index of the desired entry range.
(3) Stop Index—inclusive ending index of the desired range.

6.7.5.4.3 Outputs

(1) Start Index—inclusive starting index of the returned entry range.
(2) Stop Index—inclusive ending index of the returned range.
(3) For each Filtering Entry returned,
    (a) Address—MAC address of the desired entry.
    (b) Entry Type—either Dynamic or Static.
    (c) Either
        (i) Port Number, if the Entry Type is Dynamic, or

(ii) Port Map, as specified for the Create Static Entry operation, if the Entry Type is Static.

6.8 Bridge Protocol Entity. The Bridge Protocol Entity is described in 3.10 and Section 4.

The objects that comprise this managed resource are

(1) The Protocol Entity itself.
(2) The Ports under its control.

6.8.1 The Protocol Entity. The Protocol Entity object models the operations that can be performed upon, or inquire about, the operation of the Spanning Tree Algorithm and Protocol.

There is a single Protocol Entity per Bridge; it can, therefore, be identified as a single fixed component of the Protocol Entity resource.

The management operations that can be performed on the Protocol Entity are Read Bridge Protocol Parameters and Set Bridge Protocol Parameters.

6.8.1.1 Read Bridge Protocol Parameters

6.8.1.1.1 Purpose. To obtain information regarding the Bridge's Bridge Protocol Entity.

6.8.1.1.2 Inputs. None.

6.8.1.1.3 Outputs

(1) Bridge Identifier — as defined in 4.5.3.
(2) Time Since Topology Change — count in seconds of the time elapsed since the Topology Change flag parameter for the Bridge (4.5.3.12) was last True.
(3) Topology Change Count — count of the times the Topology Change flag parameter for the Bridge has been set (i.e., transitioned from False to True) since the Bridge was powered on or initialized.
(4) Topology Change (4.5.3.12).
(5) Designated Root (4.5.3.1).
(6) Root Cost (4.5.3.2).
(7) Root Port (4.5.3.3).
(8) Max Age (4.5.3.4).
(9) Hello Time (4.5.3.5).
(10) Forward Delay (4.5.3.6).
(11) Bridge Max Age (4.5.3.8).
(12) Bridge Hello Time (4.5.3.9).
(13) Bridge Forward Delay (4.5.3.10).
(14) Hold Time (4.5.3.14).

6.8.1.2 Set Bridge Protocol Parameters

6.8.1.2.1 Purpose. To modify parameters in the Bridge's Bridge Protocol Entity in order to force a configuration of the spanning tree and/or tune the reconfiguration time to suit a specific topology.

6.8.1.2.2 Inputs

(1) Bridge Max Age — the new value (4.5.3.8).
(2) Bridge Hello Time — the new value (4.5.3.9).
(3) Bridge Forward Delay — the new value (4.5.3.10).

(4) Bridge Priority—the new value of the priority part of the Bridge Identifier (4.5.3.7).

6.8.1.2.3 Outputs. None.

6.8.1.2.4 Procedure. The input parameter values are checked for compliance with 4.10.2. If they do not comply, or the value of Bridge Max Age or Bridge Forward Delay is less than the lower limit of the range specified in Table 4-3, then no action shall be taken for any of the supplied parameters. If the value of any of Bridge Max Age, Bridge Forward Delay, or Bridge Hello Time is outside the range specified in Table 4-3, then the Bridge need not take action.

Otherwise, the Bridge's Bridge Max Age, Bridge Hello Time, and Bridge Forward Delay parameters are set to the supplied values. The Set Bridge Priority procedure (4.8.4) is used to set the priority part of the Bridge Identifier to the supplied value.

6.8.2 Bridge Port. A Bridge Port object models the operations related to an individual Bridge Port in relation to the operation of the Spanning Tree Algorithm and Protocol.

There are a fixed set of Bridge Ports per Bridge; each can, therefore, be identified by a permanently allocated Port Identifier, as a fixed component of the Protocol Entity resource.

The management operations that can be performed on a Bridge Port are Read Port Parameters, Force Port State, and Set Port Parameters.

6.8.2.1 Read Port Parameters

6.8.2.1.1 Purpose. To obtain information regarding a specific Port within the Bridge's Bridge Protocol Entity.

6.8.2.1.2 Inputs

(1) Port Number—the number of the Bridge Port.

6.8.2.1.3 Outputs

(1) Uptime—count in seconds of the time elapsed since the Port was last reset or initialized.

(2) State—the current state of the Port (i.e., Disabled, Listening, Learning, Forwarding, or Blocking) (4.4, 4.5.5.2).

(3) Port Identifier—the unique Port identifier comprising two parts, the Port Number and the Port Priority field (4.5.5.1).

(4) Path Cost (4.5.5.3).

(5) Designated Root (4.5.5.4).

(6) Designated Cost (4.5.5.5).

(7) Designated Bridge (4.5.5.6).

(8) Designated Port (4.5.5.7).

(9) Topology Change Acknowledged (4.5.5.8).

6.8.2.2 Force Port State

6.8.2.2.1 Purpose. To force the specified Port into Disabled or Blocking.

6.8.2.2.2 Inputs

(1) Port Number—the number of the Bridge Port.

(2) State—either Disabled or Blocking (4.4, 4.5.5.2).

6.8.2.2.3 Outputs. None.

6.8.2.2.4 Procedure. If the selected state is Disabled, the Disable Port procedure (4.8.3) is used for the specified Port. If the selected state is Blocking, the

Enable Port procedure (4.8.2) is used.

6.8.2.3 Set Port Parameters

6.8.2.3.1 Purpose. To modify parameters for a Port in the Bridge's Bridge Protocol Entity in order to force a configuration of the spanning tree.

6.8.2.3.2 Inputs

(1) Port Number—the number of the Bridge Port.
(2) Path Cost—the new value (4.5.5.3).
(3) Port Priority—the new value of the priority field for the Port Identifier (4.5.5.1).

6.8.2.3.3 Outputs. None.

6.8.2.3.4 Procedure. The Set Path Cost procedure (4.8.6) is used to set the Path Cost parameter for the specified Port. The Set Port Priority procedure (4.8.5) is used to set the priority part of the Port Identifier (4.5.5.1) to the supplied value.

7. Management Protocol

This section specifies how the management facilities provided by MAC Bridges and specified in Section 6 are realized through the use of the set of management tools specified in P802.1B [3].

It specifies

(1) Use of the Network Management Protocol procedures to carry out the management operations on objects as defined in Section 6.

(2) The parameter identifiers and values associated with each operation.

(3) The encoding of parameter identifiers and value types.

NOTE: A further section is under development to specify how the management facilities provided by MAC Bridges are realized through the use of CMIS [12] and CMIP [13]. This proposed addendum will specify the ASN.1 (ISO 8824 [10]) encodings used by CMIP to convey the operations defined. It is being developed as the notational and encoding requirements for CMIP become clarified in ISO/IEC JTC1 SC21/WG4.

7.1 Specification of Operations. Each operation on an object is carried out by one of the following Network Management Operations:

(1) Get

(2) Set

(3) Action

7.1.1 Specification of a Get Operation. For each operation carried out by Get, the following are specified:

(1) For the invoke primitive and the associated Request PDU,

    (a) The Identifier Code (idCode), an integer identifying the object (parameter) to be accessed. This is referenced both by the value of the Identifier Code and by the name of the relevant ATTRIBUTE Macro call used in the ASN.1 (ISO 8824 [10]) encoding definition.

    (b) The Identifier Type (idtypeQualifier), which qualifies the Identifier Code in order to select those attributes or subordinate objects pertinent to this operation. This is referenced by the name of the relevant IDTYPE in the ATTRIBUTE Macro call (above). It is not always present.

(2) For the reply primitive and the associated Response PDU,

    (a) The Identifier Code, as specified for the corresponding invoke primitive.

    (b) The Identifier Type, as specified for the corresponding invoke primitive.

    (c) The Value Type, which conveys the result of the Get. This is referenced by the name of the relevant VALUETYPE in the ATTRIBUTE Macro call referred to above.

7.1.2 Specification of a Set Operation. For each operation carried out by Set, the following are specified:

(1) For the invoke primitive and the associated Request PDU,
    (a) The Identifier Code.
    (b) The Identifier Type, if present.
    (c) The Value Type, specifying the desired settings of the object attributes.
(2) For the reply primitive and the associated Response PDU,
    (a) The Identifier Code.
    (b) The Identifier Type.
    (c) The Value Type, which conveys the result of the Set.

7.1.3 Specification of an Action Operation. For each operation carried out by Action, the following are specified:

(1) For the invoke primitive and the associated Request PDU,
    (a) The Action Identifier — an integer identifying the action to be performed. This is referenced by the name and value of the Action Identifier Code specified in the ASN.1 (ISO 8824 [10]) encoding definition.
    (b) The Identifier Code, as for Get and Set.
    (c) The Identifier Type, as for Get and Set.
    (d) the Action Value Type, specifying the desired settings of the object attributes. This is referenced by the name of the relevant VALUETYPE in the ATTRIBUTE Macro call for the object on which the action is to be performed.
(2) For the reply primitive and the associated Response PDU,
    (a) The Action Identifier.
    (b) The Identifier Code.
    (c) The Identifier Type.

7.2 Operations. Tables 7-1, 7-2, 7-3, and 7-4 specify the mapping of the Bridge Management Operations for the Bridge Management Entity (6.4), the Forwarding Process (6.6), the Filtering Database (6.7), and the Bridge Protocol Entity (6.8) onto the Protocol Operations specified in P802.1B [3].

Table 7-1
Mapping of Bridge Management Entity Operations to Management Protocol

Management Operation	Protocol Operation	Action Identifier	Identifier Code	Identifier Type	Value Type
Discover Bridge	Get	—	bridgeEntity	BridgeSelect	BridgeConfig
Read Bridge	Get	—	bridgeEntity	—	BridgeConfig
Set Bridge Name	Set	—	bridgeEntity	BridgeNameId	BridgeName
Reset Bridge	Action	reset	bridgeEntity	—	—
Read Port	Get	—	bridgeEntity	PortId	PortConfig
Set Port Name	Set	—	bridgeEntity	PortNameId	PortName

Table 7-2
Mapping of Forwarding Process Operations to Management Protocol

Management Operation	Protocol Operation	Action Identifier	Identifier Code	Identifier Type	Value Type
Read Forwarding Port Counters	Get	—	forwardProc	PortCountsId	PortCounters
Read Transmission Priority	Get	—	forwardProc	TransmitPriorityId	TransmitPriority
Set Transmission Priority	Set	—	forwardProc	TransmitPriorityId	TransmitPriority

Table 7-3
Mapping of Filtering Database Operations to Management Protocol

Management Operation	Protocol Operation	Action Identifier	Identifier Code	Identifier Type	Value Type
Read Filtering Database	Get	—	filterDatabase	FilterDatabaseId	FilterGeneral
Set Filtering Database Ageing Time	Set	—	filterDatabase	AgeingTimeId	AgeingTime
Read Permanent Database	Get	—	filterDatabase	PermanentDatabaseId	PermGeneral
Create Filtering Entry	Action	create	filterDatabase	Entry	Filter
Delete Filtering Entry	Action	delete	filterDatabase	Entry	Filter
Read Filtering Entry	Get	—	filterDatabase	Entry	Filter
Read Filtering Entry Range	Get	—	filterDatabase	EntryRange	FilterRange

Table 7-4
Mapping of Bridge Protocol Entity Operations to Management Protocol

Management Operation	Protocol Operation	Action Identifier	Identifier Code	Identifier Type	Value Type
Read Bridge Parameters	Get	—	protocolEntity	ProtocolBridgeId	ProtocolParms
Set Bridge Parameters	Set	—	protocolEntity	BridgeParmsId	NewBridgeParms
Read Port Parameters	Get	—	protocolEntity	ProtocolPortId	PortParms
Set Port State	Action	ForceState	protocolEntity	ProtocolPortId	NewPortState
Set Port Parameters	Set	—	protocolEntity	PortParmsId	NewPortParms

132

7.3 Encoding. This section specifies the encoding of parameter identifiers and values using Abstract Syntax Notation One (ASN.1, specified in ISO 8824 [10] and ISO 8825 [11]).

```
IEEE802-1BridgeLmeDefinitions DEFINITIONS ::= BEGIN

--- rev 1

-- **** Import common definitions and assign local
--      identifiers. ****

-- Define the ATTRIBUTE macro

ATTRIBUTE ::= IEEE802CommonDefinitions.ATTRIBUTE

-- Define local names for common data types

MACAddress ::= IEEE802CommonDefinitions.MACAddress

ResourceTypeID ::= IEEE802CommonDefinitions.ResourceTypeID

-- Define Protocol Actions required (in addition to the built-in
-- Protocol Operations : Get, Set ..

IEEE802-1Bridge-Lme-ActionID ::= CHOICE {
                            privateAction [0] ANY,
                            create        [1] IMPLICIT NULL,
                            delete        [2] IMPLICT  NULL,
                            reset         [3] IMPLICIT NULL,
                            forceState    [4] IMPLICIT NULL }

-- List legal instances of Parameter Identifiers (idCodes).
-- Parameter idCodes are defined using the ATTRIBUTE macro.
-- Negative idCodes are used for implementation specific parameters.
-- The relationship between idCodes, idtypeQualifiers (IDTYPES), and
-- VALUETYPES is described along with instances of use of the ATTRIBUTE macro.
--
-- The definitions in the list here mirror those contained in the IDType
-- references in the ATTRIBUTE Macro calls.
-- NOTE: This correspondence is maintained manually, with no checking by an
-- ASN.1 compiler. The list of definitions needs to be specified here to
-- define the PDU syntax by establishing the relationship between the use
-- of the codes in the ATTRIBUTE macro, which is a notational device for
-- collecting references to a single object, and what goes in the PDU.

--


IEEE802-1Bridge-Lme-ParameterID ::= SEQUENCE {
  idCode INTEGER, -- takes vales of ATTRIBUTE codes
  idtypeQualifier CHOICE {
                bridgeSelect        [0]  IMPLICIT BridgeSelect,
                bridgeNameId        [1]  IMPLICIT BridgeNameId,
                portId              [2]  IMPLICIT PortId,
                portNameId          [3]  IMPLICIT PortNameId,
```

```
                portCountsId        [4]  IMPLICIT PortCountsId,
                transmitPriorityId  [5]  IMPLICIT TransmitPriorityId,
                filterDatabaseId    [6]  IMPLICIT FilterDatabaseId,
                ageingTimeId        [7]  IMPLICIT AgeingTimeId,
                permanentDatabaseId [8]  IMPLICIT PermanentDatabaseId,
                entry               [9]  IMPLICIT Entry,
                entryRange          [10] IMPLICIT EntryRange,
                protocolBridgeId    [11] IMPLICIT ProtocolBridgeId,
                bridgeParmsId       [12] IMPLICIT BridgeParmsId,
                protocolPortId      [13] IMPLICIT ProtocolPortId,
                portParmsId         [14] IMPLICIT PortParmsId }

-- List legal instances of Parameter Values.
-- These are the set of VALUETYPES identified  in the instances of use of
-- the ATTRIBUTE macro below.
-- The definitions in the list here mirror those contained in the
-- VALUETYPE references in the ATTRIBUTE Macro calls.
--


IEEE802-1Bridge-Lme-ParameterValue ::= CHOICE {
                resourceType     [0]  IMPLICIT ResourceTypeID,
                bridgeConfig     [1]  IMPLICIT BridgeConfig,
                bridgeName       [2]  IMPLICIT BridgeName,
                portConfig       [3]  IMPLICIT PortConfig,
                portName         [4]  IMPLICIT PortName,
                portCounters     [5]  IMPLICIT PortCounters,
                transmitPriority [6]  IMPLICIT TransmitPriority,
                filterGeneral    [7]  IMPLICIT FilterGeneral,
                ageingTime       [8]  IMPLICIT AgeingTime,
                permGeneral      [9]  IMPLICIT PermGeneral,
                filter           [10] IMPLICIT Filter,
                filterRange      [11] IMPLICIT FilerRange,
                protocolParms    [12] IMPLICIT ProtocolParms,
                portParms        [13] IMPLICIT PortParms,
                newBridgeParms   [14] IMPLICIT NewBridgeParms,
                newPortState     [15] IMPLICIT NewPortState,
                newPortParms     [16] IMPLICIT NewPortParms }

    --



-- Define manageable objects, their Parameter Identifiers (idCodes),
-- idtypeQualifiers (IDTYPES) for specifying selected attributes of the
-- object, and the Parameter Values (VALUETYPES) which are selected by
-- each IDTYPE.
--
-- These definitions follow the proforma:
--
--     objectName ATTRIBUTE
--      IDTYPES   [<IdtypeQ>] IMPLICIT AnIdtypeQualifierTypeSpecification
--                [<IdtypeQ>] IMPLICIT AnotherIdtypeQualifierTypeSpecification
--      VALUETYPES [<Valtype>] IMPLICIT AValueTypeTypeSpecification
--                [<Valtype>] IMPLICIT AnotherValueTypeTypeSpecification
--                [<Valtype>] IMPLICIT YetAnotherValueTypeTypeSpecification
--      ::= <idCode>
```

```
--
--      -- A comment expressing the relationships between the Network
--      -- Management Operations, the IDTYPES and the VALUETYPES, and the
--      -- operation of Bridge Management.
--
-- NOTE: (1) <IdtypeQ>, <Valtype>, and <idCode> are small integers,
--            e.g., "6". Each time they are used in ATTRIBUTE macros their
--            respective values are incremented by one. This applies across
--            instances of the ATTRIBUTE macro, so any <IdtypeQ> (for example)
--            is unique within the context of the IEEE802-1BridgeLmeDefinitions.
--
--        (2) There is a least one VALUETYPE for any object that can be operated
--            upon by Get or Set. There may be zero or more IDTYPES. Each
--            IDTYPE useable in a Get or Set Operation has a corresponding
--            VALUETYPE.
--
--


--
-- Define resourceTypeID

resourceTypeID ATTRIBUTE
               VALUETYPES [0] ResourceTypeID
::= 0

-- ResourceTypeID is identified by an ID of 0 in all layers.

--


-- Bridge Management Entity

bridgeEntity ATTRIBUTE
               IDTYPES    [0] BridgeSelect
                          [1] BridgeNameId
                          [2] PortId
                          [3] PortNameId
               VALUETYPES [1] BridgeConfig
                          [2] BridgeName
                          [3] PortConfig
                          [4] PortName
::= 1

--


-- The Bridge Management Entity can be accessed in the following ways:
--
--    A Get Operation specifying the idCode (1) returns BridgeConfig.
--
--    A Get Operation specifying the idCode (1) and IDTYPE BridgeSelect
--    returns BridgeConfig, provided that the Bridge's Bridge Address
--    meets the criteria for responding set out in BridgeSelect.
--
--    A Set Operation specifying the idCode, IDTYPE BridgeNameId, and VALUETYPE
--    BridgeName sets the Bridge Name.
--
```

```
--     An Action Operation with Action Identifier Reset specifying the idCode
--     resets the Bridge.
--
--     A Get Operation specifying the idCode and IDTYPE PortId returns VALUETYPE
--     PortConfig.
--
--     A Set Operation specifying the idCode, IDTYPE PortNameId, and VALUETYPE
--     PortName sets the Port Name.

--


       BridgeSelect ::= SEQUENCE {
               inclusion [0] IMPLICIT InclusionRange,
               exclusion [1] IMPLICIT ExclusionList  }

          InclusionRange ::= SET OF SEQUENCE {
                  lower [0] IMPLICIT MACAddress,
                  upper [1] IMPLICIT MACAddress }

          ExclusionList ::= SET OF MACAddress

       BridgeNameId ::= NULL

       PortId ::= INTEGER -- takes values from 1 upwards

       PortNameId ::= INTEGER -- takes same values as PortId

       BridgeConfig ::= SEQUENCE {
               bridgeAddr      [0] IMPLICIT MACAddress,
               bname           [1] IMPLICIT BridgeName,
               portAddresses   [2] IMPLICIT PortAddresses,
               uptime          [3] IMPLICIT Counter64     }

          BridgeName ::= OCTETSTRING -- printable (Latin1 String) up to 32 octets

          PortAddresses ::= SEQUENCE OF PortAddress

          PortAddress ::= SEQUENCE {
                  pNumber [0] IMPLICIT INTEGER, -- takes same values as PortId
                  portAddr [1] IMPLICIT MACAddress }

       -- BridgeName is defined above

       PortConfig ::= SEQUENCE {
               pName [0] IMPLICIT PortName,
               pType [1] IMPLICIT PortType }

          PortName ::= OCTETSTRING -- printable (Latin1 String) up to 32 octets

          PortType ::= INTEGER {
                                p802.3 (83),
                                p802.4 (84),
                                p802.5 (85) }

       -- PortName is defined above

--
```

```
-- Forwarding Process

forwardProc ATTRIBUTE
            IDTYPES     [4] PortCountsId
                        [5] TransmitPriorityId
            VALUETYPES  [5] PortCounters
                        [6] TransmitPriority
   ::= 2

--


-- The Forwarding Process can be accessed in the following ways:
--
--    A Get Operation specifying the idCode (2) and IDTYPE PortCountsId
--    returns PortCounters.
--
--    A Get Operation specifying the idCode and IDTYPE TransmitPriorityId
--    returns TransmitPriority.
--
--    A Set Operation specifying the idCode, IDTYPE TransmitPriorityId, and
--    VALUETYPE TransmitPriority sets the transmission priorities.


--


    PortCountsId ::= INTEGER -- takes values from 1 upwards, to identify Port

    TransmitPriorityId ::= INTEGER -- values from 1 upwards, to identify Port

    PortCounters ::= SEQUENCE {
            framesReceived      [0] IMPLICIT Counter64,
            discardInbound      [1] IMPLICIT Counter64,
            forwardOutbound     [2] IMPLICIT Counter64,
            discardBuffers      [3] IMPLICIT Counter64,
            discardTransitDelay [4] IMPLICIT Counter64,
            discardOnError      [5] IMPLICIT Counter64,
            details             [6] IMPLICIT DiscardDetails }

    DiscardDetails ::= SEQUENCE OF DiscardDetail

    DiscardDetail ::= SEQUENCE {
            sourceAddress [0] IMPLICIT MACAddress,
            errorReason   [1] IMPLICIT INTEGER {
                                        reasonTransmitSize (0) }}


    TransmitPriority::= SEQUENCE {
            outboundUserPriority   [0] IMPLICIT INTEGER,  -- 0 through 7
            outboundAccessPriority [1] IMPLICIT INTEGER } -- 0 through 7

--
```

137

```
-- Filtering Database

filterDatabase ATTRIBUTE
                IDTYPES      [6]   FilterDatabaseId
                             [7]   AgeingTimeId
                             [8]   PermanentDatabaseId
                             [9]   Entry
                             [10]  EntryRange
                VALUETYPES   [7]   FilterGeneral
                             [8]   AgeingTime
                             [9]   PermGeneral
                             [10]  Filter
                             [11]  FilterRange
::= 3

--



-- The Filtering Database can be accessed in the following ways:
--
--      A Get Operation specifying the idCode (3) and IDTYPE
--      FilterDatabaseId returns VALUETYPE FilterGeneral.
--
--      A Set Operation specifying the idCode, IDTYPE AgeingTimeId, and
--      VALUETYPE Ageing Time sets the filtering database ageing time.
--
--      A Get Operation specifying the idCode and IDTYPE
--      PermanentDatabaseId returns VALUETYPE PermGeneral.
--
--      An Action Operation with Action Identifier Create specifying the idCode,
--      IDTYPE Entry, and VALUETYPE Filter creates an entry in either the
--      active Filtering Database or the Permanent Database.
--
--      An Action Operation with Action Identifier Delete specifying the idCode
--      and IDTYPE Entry deletes an entry from either the active Filtering
--      Database or the Permanent Database.
--
--      A Get Operation specifying the idCode and IDTYPE Entry returns
--      VALUETYPE Filter.
--
--      A Get Operation specifying the idCode and IDTYPE EntryRange returns
--      VALUETYPE FilterRange.

--


    FilterDatabaseID ::= NULL

    PermanentDatabaseID ::= NULL

    Entry ::= SEQUENCE {
            database [0] IMPLICIT INTEGER {
                                    permanentDatabase (0),
                                    filteringDatabase (1) }
            addr     [1] IMPLICIT MACAddress }
```

```
EntryRange ::= SEQUENCE {
        database    [0] IMPLICIT INTEGER {
                                    permanentDatabase (0),
                                    filteringDatabase (1) }
        startIndex [1] IMPLICIT INTEGER,
        stopIndex  [2] IMPLICIT INTEGER }


FilterGeneral ::= SEQUENCE {
        filterSize      [0] IMPLICIT INTEGER,
        staticEntries   [1] IMPLICIT INTEGER,
        dynamicEntries  [2] IMPLICIT INTEGER,
        ageingTime      [3] IMPLICIT INTEGER }


AgeingTime ::= INTEGER


PermGeneral ::= SEQUENCE {
        permSize    [0] IMPLICIT INTEGER,
        permEntries [1] IMPLICIT INTEGER }


Filter ::= CHOICE {
        staticEntry  [0] IMPLICIT PortMaps,
        dynamicEntry [1] IMPLICIT INTEGER } -- to identify Port


    PortMaps ::= SEQUENCE OF PortMap


    PortMap ::= SEQUENCE { -- a record for every Port, ascending order
            inbound  [0] IMPLICIT INTEGER -- values from 1 to identify Port
            outbound [1] IMPLICIT BITSTRING } -- a bit for every Port,
                                            -- ascending order, True
                                            -- denoted by value 1

    FilterRange ::= SEQUENCE {
            startIndex  [0]  IMPLICIT INTEGER,
            stopIndex   [1]  IMPLICIT INTEGER,
            filterRange [2]  IMPLICIT SEQUENCE OF FilterRangeEntry }


        FilterRangeEntry ::= SEQUENCE {
                address [0] IMPLICIT MACAddress,
                filter  [1] IMPLICIT Filter }

            -- Filter is defined above


--


-- Bridge Protocol Entity

protocolEntity ATTRIBUTE
                IDTYPES    [11] ProtocolBridgeId
                           [12] BridgeParmsId
                           [13] ProtocolPortId
                           [14] PortParmsId
                VALUETYPES [12] ProtocolParms
                           [13] PortParms
                           [14] NewBridgeParms
                           [15] NewPortState
                           [16] NewPortParms
    ::= 4
```

```
--


-- The Bridge Protocol Entity can be accessed in the following ways:
--
--      A Get Operation specifying the idCode (4) and IDTYPE ProtocolBridgeId
--      returns VALUETYPE ProtocolParms.
--
--      A Set Operation specifying the idCode, IDTYPE BridgeParmsId, and
--      VALUETYPE NewBridgeParms sets Bridge Parameters.
--
--      A Get Operation specifying the idCode and IDTYPE ProtocolPortId
--      returns VALUETYPE PortParms.
--
--      An Action Operation with Action Identifier ForceState specifying
--      the idCode, IDTYPE ProtocolPortId, and VALUETYPE NewPortState forces
--      the Port to the specified State.
--
--      A Set Operation specifying the idCode, IDTYPE PortParmsId, and
--      VALUETYPE NewPortParms sets Port Parameters.
--


        ProtocolBridgeId ::= NULL

        BridgeParmsId ::= NULL

        ProtocolPortId ::= INTEGER -- takes values from 1 upwards

        PortParmsId ::= INTEGER -- takes values from 1 upwards

        ProtocolParms ::= SEQUENCE {
                bridgeid            [0]  IMPLICIT BridgeIdentifier
                timeChange          [1]  IMPLICIT INTEGER,
                topologyChangeCount [2]  IMPLICIT INTEGER,
                topologyChange      [3]  IMPLICIT BOOLEAN,
                designatedRoot      [4]  IMPLICIT BridgeIdentifier,
                rootPathCost        [5]  IMPLICIT INTEGER,
                rootPort            [6]  IMPLICIT INTEGER,
                maxAge              [7]  IMPLICIT INTEGER,
                helloTime           [8]  IMPLICIT INTEGER,
                fowardDelay         [9]  IMPLICIT INTEGER,
                bridgeMaxAge        [10] IMPLICIT INTEGER,
                bridgeHelloTime     [11] IMPLICIT INTEGER,
                bridgeForwardDelay  [12] IMPLICIT INTEGER,
                filterTime          [13] IMPLICIT INTEGER }

            BridgeIdentifier ::= OCTETSTRING       /* always length 8 */

        PortParms ::= SEQUENCE {
                state       [0] IMPLICIT PortStates,
                portid      [1] IMPLICIT PortIdentifier
                pathCost    [2] IMPLICIT INTEGER,
                desigRoot   [3] IMPLICIT BridgeIdentifier,
                desigCost   [4] IMPLICIT INTEGER,
```

140

```
            desigBridge  [5] IMPLICIT BridgeIdentifier,
            desigPort    [6] IMPLICIT PortIdentifier,
            topChangeAck [7] IMPLICIT BOOLEAN }


--


      PortStates ::= INTEGER  {
             disabled  (0),
             listening (1),
             learning  (2),
             forwarding(3),
             blocking  (4) }

      PortIdentifier ::= SEQUENCE {
             portPriority [0] IMPLICIT INTEGER,
             portNumber   [1] IMPLICIT INTEGER }

      -- BridgeIdentifier is defined above


--


  NewBridgeParms ::= SEQUENCE {
          maxAge    [0] IMPLICIT INTEGER,
          helloTime [1] IMPLICIT INTEGER,
          delay     [2] IMPLICIT INTEGER,
          priority  [3] IMPLICIT INTEGER }

  NewPortState ::= SEQUENCE {
          number    [0] IMPLICIT INTEGER,
          state     [1] IMPLICIT PortStates }

      -- PortStates is defined above

  NewPortParms ::= SEQUENCE {
          number    [0] IMPLICIT INTEGER,
          cost      [1] IMPLICIT INTEGER,
          priority  [2] IMPLICIT INTEGER }

END
```

8. Performance

This section specifies a set of parameters that represent the performance of a Bridge. These parameters have been selected to allow a basic level of confidence to be established in a Bridge, for use in an initial determination of its suitability for a given application. They cannot be considered to provide an exhaustive description of the performance of a Bridge. It is recommended that further performance information be provided and sought concerning the applicability of a Bridge implementation.

The following set of performance parameters is defined:

(1) Guaranteed Port Filtering Rate, and a related time interval T_F that together characterize the traffic for which filtering is guaranteed.

(2) Guaranteed Bridge Relaying Rate, and a related time interval T_R.

8.1 Guaranteed Port Filtering Rate.
For a specific Bridge Port, a valid **Guaranteed Port Filtering Rate**, in frames per second, is a value that, given any set of frames from the specific Bridge Port to be filtered during any T_F interval, the Forwarding Process shall filter all of the set as long as all of the following are true:

(1) The number of frames in the set does not exceed the specific Bridge Port's **Guaranteed Port Filtering Rate** multiplied by T_F.

(2) The **Guaranteed Port Filtering Rate** of each of the other Bridge Port(s) is not exceeded.

(3) The **Guaranteed Bridge Relaying Rate** is not exceeded.

(4) Relayed frames are not discarded due to output congestion (3.7.3).

8.2 Guaranteed Bridge Relaying Rate.
For a Bridge, a valid **Guaranteed Bridge Relaying Rate**, in frames per second, is a value that given any set of frames from the specific Bridge Port to be relayed during any T_R interval, the Forwarding Process shall relay all of the set as long as all of the following are true:

(1) The number of frames in the set does not exceed the Bridge's **Guaranteed Bridge Relaying Rate** multiplied by T_R.

(2) The **Guaranteed Port Filtering Rate** of each Bridge Port is not exceeded.

(3) Relayed frames are not discarded due to output congestion (3.7.3).

Appendix A
PICS Proforma

(This Appendix is a binding part of IEEE Std 802.1D-1990.)

A1. Introduction. The supplier of an implementation that is claimed to conform to IEEE Std 802.1D-1990 shall complete the following Protocol Implementation Conformance Statement (PICS) proforma and accompany it by the information necessary to identify fully both the supplier and the implementation.

A2. Abbreviations and Special Symbols: Option-status Symbols

M   Mandatory
O   Optional
On   Optional, but support of at least one of the group of options labelled by the same numeral n is required
P   Prohibited
Item: The status or answer following applies only when the PICS states that the item identified by **Item** is supported.

A3. Instructions for Completing the PICS Proforma. The PICS proforma takes the form of a fixed-format questionnaire. It allows a supplier to provide additional information of two kinds. When present, such information is to be provided as items labeled X.i or S.i for cross-referencing purposes, where i is any unambiguous identification for the item (e.g., simply a number); there are no other restrictions on its format and presentation.

A completed PICS proforma is the Protocol Implementation Conformance Statement for the implementation in question.

Answers to the questionnaire are to be provided in the right-most column, either by simply marking an answer to indicate a restricted choice (such as Yes or No), or by entering a value or a set or range of values.

Items of Exception information are required by certain answers in the questionnaire; this is indicated by an "X.__" cross-reference to be completed. This occurs when, for example, an answer indicates that a feature classified as Mandatory has not been implemented; the Exception item should contain the appropriate rationale.

The PICS allows a supplier to provide Supplementary information intended to assist the interpretation of the PICS. It is not intended or expected that a large quantity will be supplied, and a PICS can be considered complete without any such information. Examples might be an outline of the ways in which a (single) implementation can be set up to operate in a variety of environments and configurations.

References to items of Supplementary information may be entered next to any answer in the questionnaire, and may be included in items of Exception information. Supplementary information is also required by certain answers in the questionnaire where additional information is required to indicate how a feature classified as Optional has been implemented.

NOTE: Where an implementation is capable of being configured in more than one way, a single PICS may be able to describe all such configurations. However, the supplier has the choice of providing more than one PICS, each covering some subset of the implementation's configuration capabilities, in case this makes for easier and clearer presentation of the information.

A4. Identification of Requirements. The information in each of the columns labelled "Feature" in the PICS serves only to name and assist in the identification of conformance requirements in this standard. This information does not supersede or augment the provisions referenced in the main body of this standard.

PICS PROFORMA — IEEE Std 802.1D–1990

Section 1. Conformance to IEEE 802 MAC and LLC Standards

Item	Feature	Status	References	Support	
(1a)	Do the Media Access Control technologies implemented conform to the relevant MAC Standards ?	**CSMA/CD:** M **Token Bus:** M **Token Ring:** M	2.5 [5] [6] [7]	Yes Yes Yes	No: X.__ No: X.__ No: X.__
(1b)	Does the implementation of Logical Link Control conform to the LLC Standard ?	M	3.2, 3.3, 3.12, [4]	Yes	No: X.__

PICS PROFORMA — IEEE Std 802.1D–1990

Section 2. Relay and Filtering of Frames

Item	Feature	Status	References	Support	
(2a)	Are received frames with media access method errors discarded ?	M	3.5	Yes	No: X.__
(2b)	Are correctly received frames submitted to the Learning Process ?	M	3.5	Yes	No: X.__
(2c)	Are user data frames the only type of frame relayed ?	M	3.5	Yes	No: X.__
(2d)	Are request with no response frames the only frames relayed ?	M	3.5	Yes	No: X.__
(2e)	Are all frames addressed to the Bridge Protocol Entity submitted to it ?	M	3.5	Yes	No: X.__
(2f)	Are user data frames the only type of frame transmitted ?	M	3.6	Yes	No: X.__
(2g)	Are request with no response frames the only frames transmitted ?	M	3.6	Yes	No: X.__
(2h)	Are relayed frames queued for transmission only under the conditions in 3.7.1 ?	M	3.7.1, 3.9.1, 3.9.2, 4.4	Yes	No: X.__

PICS PROFORMA — IEEE Std 802.1D–1990

Section 2 (continued). Relay and Filtering of Frames

Item	Feature	Status	References	Support	
(2i)	Is the order of relayed frames of given user priority preserved ?	M	3.7.3, 3.1.1	Yes	No: X.__
(2j)	Is a relayed frame submitted to a MAC Entity for transmission only once ?	M	3.7.3, 2.3.4	Yes	No: X.__
(2k)	Is a maximum bridge transit delay enforced for relayed frames ?	M	3.7.3	Yes	No: X.__
(2l)	Are queued frames discarded if a Port leaves the Forwarding State ?	M	3.7.3	Yes	No: X.__
(2m)	Is the user priority of relayed frames preserved where possible ?	M	3.7.4, 2.3.9	Yes	No: X.__
(2n)	Is the user priority set to Outbound User Priority otherwise ?	M	3.7.4	Yes	No: X.__
(2o)	Is the access priority set to Outbound Access Priority ?	O1	3.7.4	Yes	No:
(2p)	Is the access priority set to the user priority ?	O1	3.7.4	Yes	No:

PICS PROFORMA — IEEE Std 802.1D–1990

Section 2 (continued). Relay and Filtering of Frames

Item	Feature	Status	References	Support	
(2q)	Can the Bridge use the default values of Outbound Access Priority specified ?	M	3.7.4, Table 3-2	Yes	No: X.___
(2r)	Is the undetected frame error rate greater than that achievable by preservation of the FCS where possible ?	P	3.7.5, 2.3.7	No	Yes: X.___
(2s)	Is the FCS of frames relayed between Ports of the same MAC type preserved ?	O	3.7.5	Yes	No
(3a)	Does the Bridge filter frames with equal source and destination addresses ?	O2	3.7.1, 3.7.2	Yes	No
(3b)	Does the Bridge not filter frames with equal source and destination addresses ?	O2	3.7.1, 3.7.2	Yes	No

PICS PROFORMA — IEEE Std 802.1D–1990

Section 2 (continued). Relay and Filtering of Frames

Item	Feature	Status	References	Support
(4)	Does the Bridge support management of the priority of relayed frames ?	O	3.7.4, Table 3-1, Table 3-2	Yes No S.__
(4a)	Can the Outbound User Priority be set to any of the range of values specified for each Port ?	4:M	3.7.4, Table 3-1	Yes No: X.__
(4b)	Can the Outbound Access Priority be set to any of the range of values specified for each Port ?	4:M	3.7.4, Table 3-2	Yes No: X.__

PICS PROFORMA — IEEE Std 802.1D–1990

Section 3. Maintenance of Filtering Information

Item	Feature	Status	References	Support	
(5a)	Are Filtering Database entries created and updated if and only if the Port State permits ?	M	3.8, 4.4	Yes	No: X.__
(5b)	Are Filtering Database entries made on receipt of frames with a group source address ?	P	3.8, 3.9.2	No	Yes: X.__
(5c)	Can a dynamic entry be created which conflicts with an existing static entry ?	P	3.8, 3.9	No	Yes: X.__
(5d)	Does the Filtering Database support static entries ?	M	3.9	Yes	No: X.__
(5e)	Does the Filtering Database support dynamic entries ?	M	3.9	Yes	No: X.__
(5f)	Does the creation of a static entry remove any dynamic entry for the same address ?	M	3.9	Yes	No: X.__
(5g)	Does each static entry specify a MAC Address and an outbound Port Map for each inbound Port ?	M	3.9.1	Yes	No: X.__

PICS PROFORMA — IEEE Std 802.1D–1990

Section 3 (continued). Maintenance of Filtering Information

Item	Feature	Status	References	Support	
(5h)	Are dynamic entries removed from the Filtering Database if not updated for the Ageing Time period ?	M	3.9.2	Yes	No: X.__
(5i)	Does each dynamic entry specify a MAC Address and a Port Number ?	M	3.9.2	Yes	No: X.__
(5j)	Is the Filtering Database initialised with the entries contained in the Permanent Database ?	M	3.9.3	Yes	No: X.__
(6a)	State the Filtering Database Size.	M	3.9	----	
(6b)	State the Permanent Database Size.	M	3.9	----	
(7a)	Can the Filtering Database be read by management ?	O	3.9	Yes: S.__	No
(7b)	Can the Filtering Database be updated by management ?	O	3.9	Yes: S.__	No

PICS PROFORMA — IEEE Std 802.1D-1990

Section 3 (continued). Maintenance of Filtering Information

Item	Feature	Status	References	Support	
(7c)	Can static entries be created and deleted ?	O	3.9.1	Yes: S.__	No
(7d)	Can static entries be made for individual MAC Addresses ?	7c:M	3.9.1	Yes	No: X.__
(7e)	Can static entries be made for group MAC Addresses ?	7c:M	3.9.1	Yes	No: X.__
(7f)	Can a static entry be made for the broadcast MAC Address ?	7c:M	3.9.1	Yes	No: X.__
(7g)	Can static entries be created and deleted in the Permanent Database ?	O	3.9.3	Yes: S.__	No
(8a)	Can the Bridge be configured to use the default value of Ageing Time recommended in Table 3-3 ?	O	3.9.2	Yes: S.__	No
(8b)	Can the Bridge be configured to use any of the range of values of Ageing Time specified in Table 3-3 ?	O	3.9.2	Yes: S.__	No

PICS PROFORMA — IEEE Std 802.1D–1990

Section 4. Addressing

Item	Feature	Status	References	Support	
(9a)	Can the Bridge be configured to use 48-bit Universal Addresses ?	O3	3.12	Yes: S.__	No
(9b)	Can the Bridge be configured to use 48-bit Local Addresses ?	O3	3.12	Yes: S.__	No
(9c)	Can the Bridge be configured to use 16-bit Local Addresses ?	O3	3.12	Yes: S.__	No
(10a)	Does each Port have a separate MAC Address ?	M	3.12.2	Yes	No: X.__
(10b)	Are all BPDUs transmitted to the same group address ?	M	3.12.3, 4.2	Yes	No: X.__
(10c)	Are all BPDUs transmitted to the Bridge Protocol Group Address when Universal Addresses are used ?	9a: M	3.12.3, 4.2	Yes	No: X.__

PICS PROFORMA — IEEE Std 802.1D–1990

Section 4 (continued). Addressing

Item	Feature	Status	References	Support	
(10d)	Is the source address of BPDUs the address of the transmitting Port ?	**9a:** M	3.12.3	Yes	No: X.__
(10e)	Is the Bridge Address a Universal Address ?	**9a:** M **9b:** M	3.12.5, 4.2	Yes	No
(10f)	Are frames addressed to any of the Reserved Addresses relayed by the Bridge ?	P	3.12.6	No	Yes: X.__
(11a)	Is Bridge Management accessible through each Port using the MAC Address of the Port and the LSAP assigned ?	**13:** O	3.12.4	Yes	No
(11b)	Is Bridge Management accessible through all Ports using the All LANs Bridge Management Group Address ?	**13:** O	3.12.4	Yes	No

PICS PROFORMA — IEEE Std 802.1D–1990

Section 4 (continued). Addressing

Item	Feature	Status	References	Support
(11c)	Is the Bridge Address the Address of Port 1 ?	**9a:** O **9c:** O	3.12.5	Yes No
(11d)	Are Group Addresses additional to the Reserved Addresses preconfigured in the Permanent Database ?	O	3.12.6	Yes No
(11e)	Can the additional preconfigured entries in the Filtering Database be deleted ?	**11d:** O	3.12.6	Yes No
(11f)	Are the 802.5 Functional Addresses specified in Table 3-6 preconfigured in the Permanent Database ?	**11d:** O	3.12.6	Yes No

PICS PROFORMA — IEEE Std 802.1D-1990

Section 4 (continued). Addressing

Item	Feature	Status	References	Support
(12a)	Can a group MAC Address be assigned to identify the Bridge Protocol Entity ?	**9b:** M **9c:** M	4.2	Yes No: S.__ X.__
(12b)	Can a unique identifier be assigned to the Bridge ?	**9c:** M	4.2, 4.5.3.7	Yes No: S.__ X.__
(12c)	Does each Port of the Bridge have a distinct identifier ?	M	4.2, 4.5.5.1	Yes No: X.__

PICS PROFORMA — IEEE Std 802.1D–1990

Section 5. Spanning Tree Algorithm

Item	Feature	Status	References	Support
(13a)	Are all the following Bridge Parameters maintained ?	M	4.5.3	Yes No: X.___
	Designated Root		4.5.3.1	
	Root Cost		4.5.3.2	
	Root Port		4.5.3.3	
	Max Age		4.5.3.4	
	Hello Time		4.5.3.5	
	Forward Delay		4.5.3.6	
	Bridge Identifier		4.5.3.7	
	Bridge Max Age		4.5.3.8	
	Bridge Hello Time		4.5.3.9	
	Bridge Forward Delay		4.5.3.10	
	Topology Change Detected		4.5.3.11	
	Topology Change		4.5.3.12	
	Topology Change Time		4.5.3.13	
	Hold Time		4.5.3.14	

PICS PROFORMA — IEEE Std 802.1D–1990

Section 5 (continued). Spanning Tree Algorithm

Item	Feature	Status	References	Support
(13b)	Are all the following Bridge Timers maintained ?	M	4.5.4	Yes No: X._
	Hello Timer		4.5.4.1	
	Topology Change Notification Timer		4.5.4.2	
	Topology Change Timer		4.5.4.3	
(13c)	Are all the following Port Parameters maintained for each Port ?	M	4.5.5	Yes No: X._
	Port Identifier		4.5.5.1	
	State		4.5.3.2, 4.4	
	Path Cost		4.5.5.3	
	Designated Root		4.5.5.4	
	Hello Time		4.5.5.5	
	Forward Delay		4.5.5.6	
	Bridge Identifier		4.5.5.7	
	Bridge Max Age		4.5.5.8	
	Bridge Hello Time		4.5.5.9	

PICS PROFORMA — IEEE Std 802.1D–1990

Section 5 (continued). Spanning Tree Algorithm

Item	Feature	Status	References	Support	
(13d)	Are all the following Timers maintained for each Port ?	M	4.5.6	Yes	No: X.__
	Message Age Timer		4.5.6.1		
	Forward Delay Timer		4.5.6.2		
	Hold Timer		4.5.6.3		
(13e)	Are Protocol Parameters and Timers maintained, and BPDUs transmitted, as required on each of the following events ?	M	4.7, 4.9, 4.5.3, 4.5.4, 4.5.5, 4.5.6	Yes	No: X.__
	Received Configuration BPDU		4.7.1		
	Received Topology Change Notification BPDU		4.7.2		
	Hello Timer Expiry		4.7.3		
	Message Age Timer Expiry		4.7.4		
	Forward Delay Timer Expiry		4.7.5		
	Topology Change Notification Timer Expiry		4.7.6		
	Topology Change Timer Timer Expiry		4.7.7		
	Hold Timer Expiry		4.7.8		

PICS PROFORMA — IEEE Std 802.1D–1990

Section 5 (continued). Spanning Tree Algorithm

Item	Feature	Status	References	Support	
(13f)	Do the following operations modify Protocol Parameters and Timers, and transmit BPDUs as required ?	M	4.8, 4.9, 4.5.3, 4.5.4, 4.5.5, 4.5.6	Yes	No: X.___
	Initialization		4.8.1		
	Enable Port		4.8.2		
	Disable Port		4.8.3		
	Set Bridge Priority		4.8.4		
	Set Port Priority		4.8.5		
	Set Path Cost		4.8.6		
(14a)	Does the Bridge underestimate the increment to the Message Age parameter in transmitted BPDUs ?	P	4.10.1	No	Yes: X.___
(14b)	Does the Bridge underestimate Forward Delay ?	P	4.10.1	No	Yes: X.___
(14c)	Does the Bridge overestimate the Hello Time interval ?	P	4.10.1	No	Yes: X.___

PICS PROFORMA — IEEE Std 802.1D–1990

Section 5 (continued). Spanning Tree Algorithm

Item	Feature	Status	References	Support	
(15a)	Does the Bridge use the specified value for Hold Time ?	M	4.10.2, Table 4-3	Yes	No: X.__
(16)	Does the Bridge support management of the Spanning Tree Topology ?	O	4.2	Yes	No
(16a)	Can the relative priority of the Bridge be set ?	16:M	4.2, 4.5.3.7, 4.8.4	Yes: S.__	No X.__
(16b)	Can the relative priority of the Ports be set ?	16:M	4.2, 4.5.5.1, 4.8.5	Yes: S.__	No X.__
(16c)	Can the path cost for each Port be set ?	16:M	4.2, 4.5.5.3, 4.8.6	Yes: S.__	No X.__
(17)	Does the Bridge support management of the protocol timers ?	O	4.10	Yes	No
(17a)	Can Bridge Max Age be set to any of the range of values specified ?	17:M	4.10.2, 4.5.3.8, Table 4-3	Yes: S.__	No X.__

PICS PROFORMA — IEEE Std 802.1D-1990

Section 5 (continued). Spanning Tree Algorithm

Item	Feature	Status	References	Support
(17b)	Can Bridge Hello Time be set to any of the range of values specified ?	**17:M**	4.10.2, 4.5.3.9, Table 4-3	Yes: No S.__ X.__
(17c)	Can Bridge Forward Delay be set to any of the range of values specified ?	**17:M**	4.10.2, 4.5.3.10, Table 4-3	Yes: No S.__ X.__
(18a)	Do all BPDUs contain an integral number of octets ?	M	5.1.1	Yes No: X.__
(18b)	Are all the following BPDU parameter types encoded as specified ?	M	5.1.1, 5.2	Yes No: X.__
	Protocol Identifiers		5.2.1	
	Protocol Version Identifiers		5.2.2	
	BPDU Types		5.2.3	
	Flags		5.2.4	
	Bridge Identifiers		5.2.5	
	Root Path Cost		5.2.6	
	Port Identifiers		5.2.7	
	Timer Values		5.2.8	

PICS PROFORMA — IEEE Std 802.1D–1990

Section 5 (continued). Spanning Tree Algorithm

Item	Feature	Status	References	Support	
(18c)	Do Configuration BPDUs have the format and parameters specified ?	M	5.3.1	Yes	No: X.__
(18d)	Do Topology Change Notification BPDUs have the format and parameters specified ?	M	5.3.2	Yes	No: X.__
(18e)	Are received BPDUs validated as specified ?	M	5.3.3	Yes	No: X.__

PICS PROFORMA — IEEE Std 802.1D–1990

Section 6. Bridge Management

Item	Feature	Status	References	Support	
(19)	Bridge Management Operations	O	6	Yes	No
(19a)	Discover Bridge	**19**:M	6.4.1.1	Yes	No: X.__
(19b)	Read Bridge	**19**:M	6.4.1.2	Yes	No: X.__
(19c)	Set Bridge Name	**19**:M	6.4.1.1	Yes	No: X.__
(19d)	Reset Bridge	**19**:M	6.4.1.4	Yes	No: X.__
(19e)	Read Port	**19**:M	6.4.2.1	Yes	No: X.__
(19f)	Set Port Name	**19**:M	6.4.2.2	Yes	No: X.__
(19g)	Read Forwarding Port Counters	**19**:M	6.6.1.1	Yes	No: X.__
(19h)	Read Transmission Priority	**19**:M	6.6.2.1	Yes	No: X.__
(19i)	Set Transmission Priority	**19**:M	6.6.2.2	Yes	No: X.__
(19j)	Read Filtering Database	**19**:M	6.7.1.1	Yes	No: X.__
(19k)	Set Filtering Database Ageing Time	**19**:M	6.7.1.2	Yes	No: X.__

PICS PROFORMA — IEEE Std 802.1D–1990

Section 6 (continued). Bridge Management

Item	Feature	Status	References	Support	
(19l)	Read Permanent Database	**19:**M	6.7.4.1	Yes	No: X.__
(19m)	Create Filtering Entry	**19:**M	6.7.5.1	Yes	No: X.__
(19n)	Delete Filtering Entry	**19:**M	6.7.5.2	Yes	No: X.__
(19o)	Read Filtering Entry	**19:**M	6.7.5.3	Yes	No: X.__
(19p)	Read Filtering Entry Range	**19:**M	6.7.5.4	Yes	No: X.__
(19q)	Read Bridge Protocol Parameters	**19:**M	6.8.1.1	Yes	No: X.__
(19r)	Set Bridge Protocol Parameters	**19:**M	6.8.1.2	Yes	No: X.__
(19s)	Read Port Parameters	**19:**M	6.8.2.1	Yes	No: X.__
(19t)	Force Port State	**19:**M	6.8.2.2	Yes	No: X.__
(19u)	Set Port Parameters	**19:**M	6.8.2.3	Yes	No: X.__

PICS PROFORMA — IEEE Std 802.1D-1990

Section 6 (continued). Bridge Management

Item	Feature	Status	References	Support	
(20)	IEEE 802.1 Remote Management	O	7,[3]	Yes	No
(20a)	Conformance to P802.1B*	**20:M**	[3]	Yes	No: X.__
(20b)	Network Management Operations and Encodings	**20:M**	7	Yes	No: X.__

*This provision will apply when P802.1B is approved as an IEEE standard.

PICS PROFORMA — IEEE Std 802.1D–1990

Section 7. Performance

Item	Feature	Status	References	Support
(21a)	Specify a Guaranteed Port Filtering Rate, and the associated measurement interval T_F, for each Bridge Port in the format specified below.	M	8.1	X.__
(21b)	Specify a Guaranteed Bridge Relaying Rate, and the associated measurement interval T_R, in the format specified below. Supplementary information shall clearly identify the Ports.	M	8.2	X.__

Guaranteed Bridge Relaying Rate	T_R
_____ frames per second	_____ second(s)

PICS PROFORMA — IEEE Std 802.1D–1990

Section 7 (continued). Performance

Port Number(s) or other identification	Guaranteed Port Filtering Rate (specify for all Ports)	T_F (specify for all Ports)
	_____ frames per second	_____ second(s)
	_____ frames per second	_____ second(s)
	_____ frames per second	_____ second(s)
	_____ frames per second	_____ second(s)
	_____ frames per second	_____ second(s)
	_____ frames per second	_____ second(s)
	_____ frames per second	_____ second(s)
	_____ frames per second	_____ second(s)

Appendix B
Calculating Spanning Tree Parameters

(This Appendix is not a part of IEEE Std 802.1D-1990, but is included for information only.)

This Appendix describes the method and rationale for calculating the recommended values and operational ranges for the essential Spanning Tree Algorithm performance parameters.

B1. Overview. The calculation is described in a number of steps. Each of these steps establishes values for a number of the parameters that are then used as the basis for the following steps.

The description and equations given are pertinent to a homogeneous Bridged Local Area Network, i.e., one in which all the individual LANs and Bridges are of the same type and speed. It is easy to extend this for a heterogeneous Bridged Local Area Network.

The explanation is illustrated by recommended values for IEEE 802 Local Area Networks. All times are given in seconds.

B2. Abbreviations and Special Symbols

dia	**maximum bridge diameter**
life	maximum **frame lifetime**
t_d	average frame **transit delay**
ma_d	average **medium access delay**
mma_d	**maximum medium access delay**
bt_d	**maximum bridge transit delay**
time_unit	the resolution of **Message Age**
msg_aio	**maximum Message Age increment overestimate**
msg_ao	**maximum Message Age overestimate**
pdu_d	**maximum BPDU transmission delay**
lost_msgs	maximum number of lost Bridge Protocol Messages to be tolerated prior to reconfiguration
msg_prop	**maximum Bridge Protocol Message propagation time**
hello_t	**Hello Time**
hold_t	**Hold Time**
max_age	**Max Age**
fwd_delay	**Forward Delay**

B3. Calculation

B3.1 Lifetime, Diameter, and Transit Delay

B3.1.1 Step. Choose the **maximum bridge diameter** for the Bridged Local Area Network and the **maximum bridge transit delay**. Note that, where the individual LANs support a range of transmission priorities, the bridge transit delay may vary according to priority.

B3.1.2 Basis of Choice. The **frame lifetime** is equal to the **maximum bridge diameter** times the **maximum bridge transit delay** plus the **maximum medium access delay** for the initial transmission, i.e.,

$$life = (dia \times bt\_d) + mma\_d \qquad \text{(Eq 1)}$$

The average **frame transit delay** between end systems in a Bridged Local Area Network is greater than that experienced in a single LAN by the sum of the average **forwarding delays** and **frame transmission delays** of Bridges in the path between the end systems. These will be of the order of the **medium access delays** for lightly loaded LANs. So for systems at the extremities of the Bridged Local Area Network we have the following:

$$t\_d \geq (dia \times ma\_d) + ma\_d \qquad \text{(Eq 2)}$$

This bounds our enthusiasm for insisting on low **maximum bridge transit delays** and **high maximum bridge diameters**.

B3.1.3 Recommended Values for IEEE 802 Bridged Local Area Networks

$$mma\_d \leq 0.5$$
$$life \leq 7.5$$
$$dia = 7$$
$$bt\_d = 1.0$$

B3.2 Transmission of BPDUs

B3.2.1 Step. Select the transmission priority for BPDUs and a value for the **maximum BPDU transmission delay**.

B3.2.2 Basis of Choice. In general, a high transmission priority will be chosen, since the continued operation of the Bridged Local Area Network depends on the successful transmission and reception of BPDUs. In some cases, other traffic native to an individual LAN may be more important.

The lowest value that could be chosen for the **maximum BPDU transmission delay** then is the **maximum medium access delay** for frames of that priority. In recognition of implementation difficulties that may arise in trying to achieve this figure, it seems more reasonable to choose the value to be equal to the **maximum bridge transit delay** for frames transmitted with that priority.

$$pdu\_d = bt\_d \qquad \text{(Eq 3)}$$

B3.2.3 Recommended Values for IEEE 802 Bridged Local Area Networks. Priority transmission is not available for all IEEE 802 media access methods. Therefore, we select the following:

$$pdu\_d = bt\_d$$
$$= 1.0$$

B3.3 Accuracy of Message Age

B3.3.1 Step. Select an appropriate value for the **maximum Message Age increment overestimate**.

This is the maximum overestimate of the increment made to the value of the Message Age parameter in transmitted Bridge Protocol Data Units. This parameter allows a Bridge receiving a Protocol Message to discard the information in it when it becomes too old. The transmitting Bridge should not be allowed to underestimate the value of this field.

Calculate the value of the **maximum Message Age overestimate**, which is the maximum overestimate any Bridge can make of the age of received Bridge Protocol Message information.

B3.3.2 Basis of Choice. The choice of **maximum Message Age increment overestimate** is governed by the following:

(1) *time_unit* — the resolution with which the Message Age parameter is carried in Configuration Messages.
(2) The granularity and accuracy of timers in the Bridge.
(3) The **maximum BPDU transmission delay**.

Assuming the Bridge timers are not necessarily synchronized with received BPDUs, that they are accurate, and that they have a granularity of *time_unit*, we have, as a best effort, the following:

$$msg\_aio = pdu\_d + time\_unit \tag{Eq 4}$$

This value should be rounded up to the nearest multiple of *time_unit*. It is worth noting here that any Bridge will always increment the value by at least one unit.

Making the same allowance for the timers in a Bridge receiving and storing Bridge Protocol Message information, the **maximum Message Age overestimate** will be equal to the **maximum Message Age increment overestimate** times the **maximum bridge diameter** minus one:

$$msg\_ao = msg\_aio \times (dia - 1) \tag{Eq 5}$$

B3.3.3 Recommended Values for IEEE 802 Bridged Local Area Networks

$msg\_aio = 1.0$
$msg\_ao = 6.0$

B3.4 Hello Time

B3.4.1 Step. Provisionally select a value for the Hello Time.

B3.4.2 Basis of Choice. The choice of Hello Time is made with regard to its contribution to the **maximum Bridge Protocol Message propagation time** (see next step).

There is no point in transmitting Bridge Protocol Messages at intervals more frequent than the **maximum BPDU transmission delay**. In the worst case, where we are trying to guarantee correct operation, these messages would just run into one another.

A provisional value of twice the **maximum BPDU transmission delay** is suggested.

$$hello\_t = 2 \times pdu\_d \tag{Eq 6}$$

B3.4.3 Recommended Values for IEEE 802 Bridged Local Area Networks

$hello\_t = 2.0$

B3.5 Bridge Protocol Message Propagation

B3.5.1 Step. Calculate the **maximum Bridge Protocol Message propagation time**.

B3.5.2 Basis of Choice. The **maximum Bridge Protocol Message propagation time** is the maximum time taken for a Bridge Protocol Message information to cross the Bridged Local Area Network, from Bridge to Bridge. This is composed of the following components:

(1) The maximum propagation time for a single Bridge Protocol Message to cross the Bridged Local Area Network, i.e., **maximum BPDU transmission delay** times the **maximum bridge diameter** minus one.

(2) An allowance of **Hello Time** times the maximum number of consecutive lost Bridge Protocol Messages to be tolerated (note that losing even a single message should be a rare occurrence).

(3) A further allowance of **Hello Time**, since we should not assume synchronization with the Root Bridge, and we may have to wait that long for it to transmit the next BPDU.

$$msg\_prop = ((lost\_msgs + 1) \times hello\_t) + pdu\_d \times (dia - 1) \qquad \text{(Eq 7)}$$

B3.5.3 Recommended Values for IEEE 802 Bridged Local Area Networks. Assuming $lost\_msgs = 3$,

$msg\_prop = 14.0$

B3.6 Hold Time

B3.6.1 Step. Select a value for **Hold Time**.

B3.6.2 Basis of Choice. If **Hold Time** is greater than the **maximum BPDU transmission delay**, then the **Maximum Bridge Protocol Message propagation time** will be set, in the worst scenario, by a delay of **Hold Time** at each Bridge rather than by a delay of **maximum BPDU transmission delay**. This would invalidate the conclusion in B3.5, above. We therefore choose the following:

$$hold\_t = pdu\_d \qquad \text{(Eq 8)}$$

B3.6.3 Recommended Values for IEEE 802 Bridged Local Area Networks

$hold\_t = 1.0$

B3.7 Max Age

B3.7.1 Step. Calculate the lower limit for **Max Age** for the Bridged Local Area Network.

B3.7.2 Basis of Choice. Under stable conditions (i.e., no failure, removal or insertion of Bridges and other LAN components), Bridges on the periphery of Bridged Local Area Network must not time out the Root. To do so would result in temporary local denial of service.

This means that **Max Age** must be adequate to cope with the worst-case propagation delays and Protocol Message Age inaccuracies as follows.

If at any time a Bridge is depending on Protocol Message information whose age has been maximally overestimated, then the sum of

(1) The interval between the transmission of the next Protocol Message that it receives from the Root and the original transmission of the Protocol Message information it is currently using —
(2) The overestimate of the Age of the current information —
(3) The propagation time of the next Protocol Message to be received —

must be less than Max Age, or the Bridge will timeout the Protocol Message information and attempt to become the Root itself.

$$max\_age = ((lost\_msgs + 1) \times hello\_t) + msg\_ao + (pdu\_d \times (dia - 1))$$
$$= msg\_ao + msg\_prop \qquad \text{(Eq 9)}$$

B3.7.3 Recommended Values for IEEE 802 Bridged Local Area Networks

$max\_age = 20.0$

B3.8 Forward Delay

B3.8.1 Step. Calculate the **Forward Delay**.

B3.8.2 Basis of Choice. When the Forward Delay Timer for a Port expires and the Bridge starts forwarding received frames on that Port, we must be sure that there are no longer any frames in the system that were being forwarded on the previous **active topology**. If there are, then we run the risk of duplicating frames or, if remnants of the old **active topology** still exist while we move to the new topology, of creating data loops.

So the Listening and Learning periods during which the Forward Delay Timer runs must cover the following consecutive periods:

(1) From the first Bridge Port entering the Listening State (and staying there through the subsequent reconfiguration) to the last Bridge in the Bridged Local Area Network hearing of the change in **active topology**.
(2) For the last Bridge to stop the forwarding of frames received on the previous topology and for the last frame so forwarded to disappear.

In (1), above, there may be a difference of up to **maximum Message Age overestimate** in the times at which Bridges timeout old Root information and are prepared to become or listen to a new Root. Following this, it can take **maximum Bridge Protocol Message propagation time** for the news of the new topology to propagate from the new Root to all Bridges.

For (2), above, the time to stop forwarding will be the **maximum transmission halt delay**, which is bounded by the maximum bridge transit delay (for all priorities); subsequently, the frame will disappear within the frame lifetime.

So we have the following:

$$2 \times fwd\_d \geq msg\_ao + msg\_prop + bt\_d + life \qquad \text{(Eq 10)}$$

B3.8.3 Recommended Values for IEEE 802 Bridged Local Area Networks

$fwd\_d = 15.0$

B4. Selection of Parameter Ranges

B4.1 Absolute Maximum Values. It might be desirable to configure a LAN or Bridge with a greater **maximum medium access delay** than assumed in the calculations for recommended values above. This could be a consequence of the type of traffic carried by the LAN or particular aspects of a Bridge implementation, designed to maximize the throughput, for example. However, it is highly desirable that absolute maximum values of **maximum bridge transit delay**, **maximum BPDU transmission delay**, and **maximum Message Age increment overestimate** be mandated by this IEEE Standard in order to provide for interoperability.

A Bridge operating with absolute maximum values of these parameters should be configurable with Bridges employing recommended values in a Bridged Local Area Network of a **bridge diameter** of at least 3. This criterion is met by the following:

$$bt\_d \leq 2.0$$
$$pdu\_d \leq 2.0$$
$$msg\_aio \leq 2.0$$

These limits are believed to encompass the requirement for parameter values greater than those recommended in B3.

B4.2 Hold Time. There is no benefit in reducing **Hold Time** below the recommended value of **maximum BPDU transmission delay**. Nor would any purpose be served, in terms of reduced use of bandwidth or processing capability in a Bridge, by increasing **Hold Time**. It is, therefore, appropriate to fix the value of this parameter as a constant:

$$hold\_t = 1.0$$

B4.3 Range of Hello Time. There is no requirement for **Hello Time** to be less than **Hold Time**. Similarly, no purpose would be served by setting **Hello Time** to more than twice the absolute maximum value for **maximum BPDU transmission delay**. Therefore we choose the following:

$$1.0 \leq hello\_t \leq 4.0$$

B4.4 Maximum Required Values of Max Age and Forward Delay. The maximum required values for **Max Age** and **Forward Delay** are calculated using the equations of B3 with the following parameter values:

$$dia = 7$$
$$mma\_d \leq 2.0$$
$$bt\_d = 2.0$$
$$pdu\_d = 2.0$$
$$msg\_aio = 2.0$$
$$hello\_t = 4.0$$
$$lost\_msgs = 3$$

which gives the following:

$$max\_age \leq 40.0$$
$$fwd\_delay \leq 30.0$$

Although these are believed to be the maximum values required there is no desire to prevent greater values being used.

B4.5 Minimum Values for Max Age and Forward Delay. The minimum realistic values for **Max Age** and **Forward Delay** are calculated using the equations of B3 with the following parameter values:

$$dia\ =\ 2$$
$$mma\_d\ \le\ 0.5$$
$$bt\_d\ =\ 0.5$$
$$pdu\_d\ =\ 0.5$$
$$hold\_t\ =\ 1.0$$
$$msg\_aio\ =\ 1.0$$
$$hello\_t\ =\ 1.0$$
$$lost\_msgs\ =\ 3$$

which gives the following:

$$max\_age\ \ge\ 6.0$$
$$fwd\_delay\ \ge\ 4.0$$

It is suggested that Bridge implementations do not permit lower values of **Max Age** and **Forward Delay** to be used in order to guard against absurd settings.

B4.6 Relationship Between Max Age and Forward Delay. In order to further guard against bad settings of parameters that affect the correctness of operation of the Spanning Tree Algorithm and Protocol, it is suggested that Bridges enforce the relationship between **Max Age** and **Forward Delay** given in B3.8 by ensuring that

$$2 \times (fwd\_delay - 1.0)\ \ge\ max\_age$$